Vision and Value
in Health Information

Edited by

Michael Rigby

Reader in Health Planning and Management
Keele University

Radcliffe Medical Press

Radcliffe Medical Press Ltd
18 Marcham Road
Abingdon
Oxon OX14 1AA
United Kingdom

www.radcliffe-oxford.com
The Radcliffe Medical Press electronic catalogue and online ordering facility.
Direct sales to anywhere in the world.

British Library Cataloguing in Publication Data

A catalogue record for this book is available from the British Library.

ISBN 1 85775 863 3

Typeset by Aarontype Ltd, Easton, Bristol
Printed and bound by TJ International Ltd, Padstow, Cornwall

A tribute to the inspiration of Edith Körner

Contents

Foreword

It gives me great pleasure to write the foreword to this series of essays on innovation in the presentation and use of information in healthcare. Throughout my career, and not least in my current position as Chair of the Commission for Health Improvement (CHI), I have found that recognising the importance of information, innovation and investment in its use, is key to determining success or failure.

As an undergraduate and postgraduate student of medicine in Wales I had the privilege of being taught by one of the most innovative thinkers in the information field, Archie Cochrane, who as Director of the MRC Epidemiology Unit in Cardiff, became a legend in his own right in pioneering a rigorous scientific approach to information and evidence. That legacy lives on, quite rightly, in the Cochrane collaboration that was inspired by his approach and named not so much in his honour as because the very citation of his name encapsulates the vision and the standards. And in a different but not unrelated way, Julian Tudor Hart was bringing a rigorous approach to record-keeping and data capture to general practice in Glyncorrwg, in a way which inspired a very industrial practice population, as well as demonstrating how to address the Inverse Care Law that he identified. So as a result, healthcare delivery in South Wales was very much influenced by this recognition of information and establishment of innovation in its application.

In my own early practice in community medicine, aspects of information were key both in terms of providing best evidence, but – in a sense more importantly – in terms of recording local service availability and individual patient need. And so with my progression to Chief Medical Officer for Wales, it was only natural that information should be a key resource which I valued and nourished. We were able to watch what was happening not only in England but elsewhere, and to interpret and adapt those initiatives to apply them to the specific challenges of the Principality. At the same time, though, we sought to put great emphasis upon innovative and successful completion of information investment, rather than merely the initial pioneering idea. These were exciting times, with the Strategies for Health Gain just one significant example. These were firmly grounded in information – information as to need, information as to performance, but above all setting measurable indices of progress counted in terms of measured benefit to the population.

The technical infrastructure to obtain and use good-quality data was not overlooked either. One particular achievement was the Digital All Wales Network (DAWN), which rolled out to the whole of the NHS family throughout Wales, including primary care, the benefits of a dedicated health infrastructure. This was later followed by developments such as the private intranet, Cymru-Web. We also placed importance in investing in an information-handling resource, best known as the Health Intelligence Unit, which later developed into Health Solutions Wales.

One of the other major initiatives I had the challenge of working on, together with Sir Kenneth Calman in England, was the total review of cancer services in England and Wales. This was a challenging brief, and our recommendations were equally challenging to those practising in this important field throughout England and Wales. That we called for a radical reshaping of service provision is now well known, and the rationale for this was entirely evidence-based. It was upon review of information about activity and results that we were able to reach the conclusions we did, motivate so many organisations and individuals to undertake difficult change with comparative smoothness, and as a result, bring about lasting benefits to the population and patients.

From within Wales we were not directly involved in the work of the Steering Group on Health Services Information, and the drive of Mrs Körner. However, as with many other innovations in England, we watched with a mixture of envy and relief, but above all with the great opportunity of learning from observation. Indeed, on a fine day Mrs Körner's home region could be viewed across the water from my own constituency! The challenges that the Steering Group faced were clearly major, both in terms of the size of the task and in terms of the natural institution of organisational inertia through the long tradition of the pre-existing statistical systems. But what was clear was that Edith Körner bought a combination of vision, inspiration and sheer determination which motivated her Steering Group, charmed and persuaded the wider constituency, and drove her immediate support team. From her work came a vision, and then a demonstration, of how to harness modern management approaches to information as a resource and apply them to the huge and technically precise domain of health information.

Now, in my current position as Chair of the CHI, I continue to be very convinced of the importance of information in healthcare management and clinical practice. In our work in the CHI we see innovation and good practice; inevitably, we also have to focus on the more disappointing areas of poor practice and other problems. And if I were asked to identify any particular factors which seem to differentiate between success and failure, I have to say that nearly all the locations where we have to deal with problems can be identified as those with either poor information systems, or scant understanding of how to use that information in a diagnostic and material way. And similarly, with nearly every example of good practice can be seen investment in information, which is a key factor.

So it therefore gives me great pleasure to welcome and introduce this set of essays on the innovative use and development of information in healthcare. Firstly, because I think it rightly acknowledges and pays tribute to the work of one of the key visionaries in this field, Edith Körner, who in line with many other pioneers was not fully recognised or appreciated at the time. And secondly, because I think it is important that we continue to innovate and develop our information-handling abilities, and this collection comprises a number of very different but equally important visionary approaches and applications described by colleagues whose work is well known to and highly respected by me.

I hope that you enjoy reading these as much as I did. More importantly, I hope that this collection inspires further practical use of information in healthcare. The production of this volume is an important initiative by the Nuffield Trust, and I welcome it.

Dame Deirdre Hine
President Royal Society of Medicine
July 2003

Preface

Edith Körner: analyst and visionary

Perhaps once in a lifetime, if one is lucky, one is privileged to encounter the influence of an individual who combines vision, analysis and commitment in a way that commands respect whilst providing inspiration. Edith Körner was such a memorable person.

Edith Körner arrived in this country with little choice, as a pre-war refugee. In modern parlance, she would be classed as an asylum-seeker, arriving on her own as a homeless teenager unable to speak English. She proceeded in due course to give to her adopted country an input and legacy that multiply rewarded that initial asylum and hospitality.

This volume reflects on merely one facet of her public service contribution in Great Britain. There were earlier and later phases in very different spheres, which makes her contribution all the more impressive. And of course there were roles as supportive wife and caring mother fitted in as well, indeed first and foremost.

However, for that small group who had the opportunity of working with Edith Körner in seeking to develop systematic health information, this was a privilege and an inspiration. And for the much wider NHS community, who even 20 years later use her name daily as a term describing specific information concepts, she has by definition become something of a legend. Few can have their work endure in this way, even if the amount of achievement made was far less than she wished and hoped.

This volume is not a retrospective study, though contributions start with an analysis of her work – one by a contemporary and one by a retrospective discoverer of a legacy deeper than is usually appreciated. Rather, the intention is to pay tribute to Edith Körner's skills and vision by seeking, however modestly, to continue that visionary thinking along different new strands in a way that, regrettably, is usually excluded in the modern task-driven and problem-orientated public sector.

What were the magic ingredients that enabled Edith Körner not only to be so successful with her initial daunting task, but to lead others to want to build on it? Working with her was to experience a clarity of thought, and a depth of analysis, that were powerful and enlightening at the same time. She not only had a mental master plan for her work, but she was active in small group discussions of every detail. With her at the table the debate was always friendly, and tolerant of exploratory ideas, yet any unfounded assumption or unjustified conclusion was pounced on for what it was – unsustainable. The precise tones of the accent with its surviving hint of east-European origins would pose the question that, though not strictly rhetorical, by its very asking provided the answer. The careful phraseology, the momentary pause to produce every time the absolutely apt word or phrase, taught many of us a new level of analytic and reflective discussion. Yet this was always amicable, and business meetings were like (indeed were) meetings of friends to which one always looked forward.

And to the work itself, Mrs Körner brought the background experience of being the vice chair of a regional health authority, and therefore strong awareness of the issues and challenges of obtaining adequate information for strategic management. Yet, in modern parlance, she was a 'bottom up' as much as a 'top down' person. Running throughout her reports was the express principle that it was difficult to think of any information item or analysis that was relevant at a higher level if it was not relevant at the level below it. This was true respect for those undertaking the operational work of the NHS, whilst also recognising the need for modern management of an informed nature, in rather the way which was articulated a decade later by Sir Roy Griffiths.

The freshness of Edith Körner's approach – the legacy upon which this volume seeks to build – was not framed in specific recommendations and reports, important though they were at the time and in many ways still continue to have influence. Rather, it was the important recognition of information as a key management tool, with its concomitant need to apply consistent objective principles and methods in the NHS to its recording, gathering and use that was the beacon. The reports of her steering group start with an analysis of the requirements for information, and many of the concepts she described were articulated in ways well ahead of their time. The terms 'health gain' or 'cost-effectiveness' may not have been current at the time, but those underlying concepts can clearly be seen in the arguments expressed. Alistair Mason, who provides our first contribution, was the secretary to the Steering Group, and therefore worked with Edith Körner closely on a daily basis. My own role at the time was much more humble, as a mere co-optee to one working group, but the fact that we were both treated in the same way, and both have the same warm yet respectful recalls, is itself an example of Edith Körner's inspiring openness and inclusiveness in every sense of the word.

The great disappointment of Edith Körner's work was that it never reached true fruition. Very seldom does the public service, not least the NHS organisation, have capacity for a visionary. Mrs Körner started off along an important road towards the development of effective purposeful information systems; the powers that be decided that her first, interim, reports were perfectly adequate as the final answer. For them the future was for others, and so not their responsibility. Edith Körner and her immediate colleagues were bitterly disappointed; the NHS and healthcare have suffered seriously as a result. I hope this volume provides a modest opportunity to give visionary thinking an appropriate outlet.

However, Edith Körner's work, although refreshingly clear and objective, was neither cold nor divorced from real life. That, indeed, is part of the endearing richness of the example she left. It is important not to let leading-edge thinking, nor top-level national responsibilities, become either remote or cold. Those who worked with Edith Körner will each have a favourite personal anecdote.

One legend concerns a time when Mrs Körner was invited to speak to the young members' branch of a national professional organisation. After the formal proceedings, Mrs Körner made it clear that she preferred to socialise with the young members rather than the platform party. Someone diffidently invited her to join the table tennis party, which she willing accepted, and play commenced in a gentle style with due respect for the dignity of their older guest. Sometime later, when the visiting speaker had thoroughly trounced all the young members, she gently asked whether they were unaware that she had been a youth champion in the country of her birth. Like her cognitive skills, this physical performance was little diminished with age.

A quite separate anecdote relates to the time, in the midst of the full flurry of the work of the steering group, when, after a strenuous week, a relaxing weekend was clearly deserved and needed. However, on subsequently enquiring whether rest and recreation had indeed been the order of the weekend, the reply was that she had completed some home plumbing. When those present argued that this was not what was planned or appropriate, her comment was archetypical of the lady, *'The job had to be done and no plumber was available. So I thought of the IQ of a plumber, I thought of my IQ, and wondered why I was waiting and then going to pay a large sum of money, so I went out and bought a book and did the job myself.'* This was not in any way an anti-tradesman statement, but rather a philosophy that if something needed doing the central duty was to acquire the skills and do the job, and not to consider any essential task demeaning.

Those two anecdotes encapsulate the humanitarian inspiration which Edith Körner provided. She was able to mix and enjoy the company of anyone, and to tackle any necessary task, but in both cases to do them with good grace, to a high standard, and above all, with enjoyment.

Edith Körner may have been ahead of her time, or conversely the times may not have been ready for her. She brought a blend of experience, common sense, rigorous analysis and vision to an important task, and that is a powerful mixture that serves as a model framework. She may not have finished her task as she saw it, or indeed as others hoped it would be undertaken, but there is no doubt that she left a legacy – both of practice and of principle – that has endured. These are important lessons for the future of health information – to have objectivity, clarity and vision; to recognise the skills and the humanity of those delivering care at the operational level; and at the same time to recognise the importance of accurate and timely management information derived from operational data. Those principles may have been overshadowed by political expediency in aspects of recent policy, which has itself proved far less enduring, but their appropriateness is shown by the fact that they can be recognised as themes in each of the papers in this collection.

Michael Rigby
Reader in Health Planning and Management
Keele University
July 2003

About the editor

Michael Rigby BA FSS
Reader
Centre for Health Planning and Management, Keele University
Michael Rigby's initial career was in the National Health Service, commencing as a researcher for the then Cheshire County Council Health Department. He progressed through information, planning, and computer records positions in Cheshire Area Health Authority, culminating in appointment as Regional Service Planning Officer for Mersey Regional Health Authority. Within this period he was a member of the Community Services Working Group of the Steering Group on Health Services Information, chaired by Mrs Körner. He then moved to the Centre for Health Planning and Management as Lecturer, with special interests in information and related systems, healthcare reform, and non-acute services. He teaches and leads courses on the two MBA programmes and other programmes run by the Centre, and undertakes a range of research projects on information issues in health and healthcare policy and practice. He has a wide range of publications, is founding editor of the *Harnessing Health Information* series with Radcliffe Medical Press, and lead editor of *Taking Health Telematics into the 21st Century*, also from Radcliffe Medical Press with support from the Nuffield Trust.

About the contributors

Dr Mitch Blair MBBS BSc MSc FRCPCH FRCP FRIPH
Consultant Reader in Paediatrics and Child Public Health, Imperial College
Mitch Blair trained in London as a paediatrician, then moved to Nottingham as Senior Lecturer in Community Paediatrics from 1990 to 1998. There he developed his interest in the role of information systems in supporting child health. He co-chaired the Royal College of Paediatrics and Child Health Interprofessional Forum on Child Health Informatics. He is currently an academic clinical paediatrician working at Northwick Park Hospital and active member of the National Child Health Informatics Consortium, and has continued to influence local and national policy on child public health through his teaching and research. The original Körner reports have remained an important influence throughout his career.

Professor Dame June Clark BA MPhil PhD RN RHV FRCN
Emeritus Professor of Community Nursing, University of Wales Swansea
Visiting Professor, University of Iowa, USA
Visiting Professor, University of Maribor, Slovenia
June Clark worked in the NHS for 35 years as a health visitor, Director of Community Nursing Services and Chief Nurse to a Health Authority before moving into higher education in 1990. Her special interest is the development of a minimum data set and standardised terminology to describe nursing in patient records. She has acted as consultant to the International Council of Nurses and to the World Health Organization, and has held many leadership positions in nursing including President of the Royal College of Nursing 1990–94. She is a Non-executive Director of Carmarthenshire NHS Trust.

Professor Don E Detmer MD MA FAAAS FACMI FACS
Dennis Gillings Professor of Health Management, University of Cambridge
Professor Emeritus and Professor of Medical Education, University of Virginia, USA
Don Detmer practiced as a vascular and sports medicine surgeon for 25 years and also developed the first Masters level management and leadership educational

programme for clinician executives in the USA (University of Wisconsin-Madison 1973–84), as well as administering two academic health science centres (Universities of Utah and Virginia 1984–95). A lifetime associate of the National Academies, he has been active in health policy in Washington DC, having chaired the Board of Regents of the National Library of Medicine, the National Committee on Vital and Health Statistics, and the Board on Health Care Services of the Institute of Medicine. He has been instrumental in the development of the National Health Information Infrastructure in the USA. He has directed Cambridge University Health for the past four years.

Dr JA Muir Gray CBE MD
Director of the National electronic Library for Health
Director of National Screening Programmes
Institute of Health Sciences, Oxford
Muir Gray's main interest has for many years been getting research into practice.

Dr Azim Lakhani MA FFPHM
Director of the National Centre for Health Outcomes Development (NCHOD)
Azim Lakhani is an accredited specialist in public health medicine. He was previously Director of Public Health for West Lambeth Health Authority, subsequently a Principal Medical Officer and Director of the Central Health Outcomes Unit of the Department of Health. Alongside overall current responsibility for NCHOD's research and development work concerning various aspects of health outcomes assessment, Azim works directly on the development and production of some 150 clinical and health indicators used by the National Health Service in England (*Compendium of Clinical and Health Indicators*) plus dissemination of information on health outcomes via an NHS website – the *Clinical and Health Outcomes Knowledge Base*.

Dr Alastair Mason FRCP (London) FFPHM
Consultant Epidemiologist
National Centre for Health Outcomes Development
Alastair Mason was Secretary to the Steering Group on Health Services Information for its duration. He was Regional Public Health Director of the South Western RHA from 1987 to 1994. He is currently a freelance public health consultant with part-time appointments with the National Centre for Health Outcomes Development and the Royal College of Physicians Clinical Effectiveness and Evaluation Unit. He edited the volume of essays, published by the King's Fund to honour Mrs Körner, *Walk don't Run*.

Jeannette Murphy BSc DipComputing
Senior Lecturer in Health Informatics
**Centre for Health Informatics and Multiprofessional Education (CHIME), Royal
Free and University College Medical School, London**
Jeanette Murphy's special interest is in demystifying health informatics so that
doctors, nurses, managers and administrative staff can see its relevance to their
work and to patient care; she is also interested in understanding why information systems do and do not deliver benefits. She does this as Graduate Tutor in
CHIME, with overall responsibility for matters relating to education, training
and professional development. She oversees research degree students and two
MSc programmes (Clinical Risk Management and Health Informatics). Jeanette
is also a visiting lecturer at St George's Hospital Medical School (a Health Informatics module), Keele University Postgraduate Medical School and the School
of Pharmacy (University of London). She organises IT skills training for medical
students, and special study modules in health informatics. When she was
initially trying to understand the challenges facing the NHS in relation to information management she chanced upon the 'Körner Reports', and the breadth
and vision of this work shaped her understanding of what we now call health
informatics, and influenced her career.

Dr Harry Rutter MA MB BChir MSc MFPH
Specialist Registrar, South East Public Health Observatory
Fellow, Department of Public Health, Oxford University
Harry Rutter worked in a range of clinical jobs before training in public health.
He is interested in sustainability, transport and health, and the impact of tech-
nology and communications on the way in which we practice as professionals.

Professor Ellie Scrivens BA PhD
**Professor of Health Policy and Director of the NHS Controls Assurance Support
Unit**
Keele University, Staffordshire
Ellie Scrivens is Professor of Health Policy at Keele University and Director of
the Controls Assurance Support Unit – a national Department of Health-funded
unit to promote risk management and improved control systems within the
NHS. She is also Vice-Chair of Shropshire and Staffordshire Strategic Health
Authority, a member of the accreditation panel for the Scottish Prison Service,
is on the board of a number of NHS national organisations concerned with standards and quality of healthcare, and is consultant to the Department of Health
on the development of national standards for healthcare. She was a member of
the Community Services Working Group of the Steering Group on Health Services. She has written extensively on quality in healthcare, and with Professor
Rudolf Klein contributed to *Walk don't Run*, the first volume of essays devoted to
Edith Körner's work.

Peter Tiplady MB BS MRCGP FFPHM
Honorary Consultant in Public Health Medicine, Cumbria and Lancashire Strategic Health Authority
Formerly Director of Public Health, North Cumbria Health Authority
Peter Tiplady recently retired after 30 years in public health, but continues with a number of professional and charitable voluntary activities. He has had a career-long interest in information for health, in which his special interests included information for child health and community health services. More recently he has been concerned with the epidemiology of diabetes, issues of foot and mouth disease, complementary healthcare and medical ethics. His published and current research include Section 47 of the NHS Act, radioiodine thyroid cancer in Cumbria, foot and mouth disease, control of diabetes during the foot and mouth disease epidemic (in progress) and evaluation of healing by light touch. He was Vice Chair of Working Group 'D' (community services information) of the Steering Group on Health Services Information.

Professor John G Williams MA MSc FRCP
Professor of Health Services Research, Clinical School, University of Wales Swansea
Consultant Gastroenterologist, Bro Morgannwg NHS Trust
John Williams has a longstanding interest in improving the availability, utility and validity of information for patient care and service management. He is Director of the Royal College of Physicians' Health Informatics Unit, which is promoting the education and culture change needed amongst physicians, and developing evidence-based standards for medical records. He has a particular interest in the routine capture of patient-focused outcomes and in the use of routine data for service planning and research.

Introduction

This publication, *Vision and Value in Health Information*, not only celebrates the contribution of Edith Körner over the years but also offers a significant challenge for a proper place for health information in the modernisation of health services in the UK.

The Nuffield Trust, in its *Policy Futures for UK Health*[1] project, was attempting to analyse the broad environment for health in this country in the year 2015, and the implications of that for current UK health policy. The trust indicated some areas where the government could take action now in order to anticipate the likely circumstances of 2015. This time frame was chosen carefully with a view to making a constructive contribution to policy development and not creating a piece of abstract futurology. The period under review extended beyond the usual constraint of the electoral cycle but was short enough to allow a realistic assessment of future developments.

The report was in the Nuffield Trust tradition of stimulating change in the culture of the health policy-making process, and of encouraging thinking and analysis based on evidence. There were three messages to the prime minister:

- not to forget the issue of health while reforming the NHS
- how to manage public expectations and to pay for them
- the importance of thinking through fully and well in advance the implications of change for the people who work in the health service.

The study foresaw very radical new developments in, among other things, information and communication technology, that would move conventional professional boundaries within the workforce and change the locations of care. All three areas highlighted that an effective policy for information and information technology (IT) was essential. No business runs on as little information or IT expertise and capability as does the NHS, or has invested so little in general staff training or in raising awareness of the importance of data, information and intelligence. Unless information is properly gathered, organised, analysed and used, the NHS will continue to lack some of the most basic tools of policy-making and may be unable to cope with the changes that lie ahead, still less with moderate public expectations in relation to them.

Central to stimulating debate on the problems that we now face and will face in the future, the Nuffield Trust is pursuing its interest in benchmarking.

A great deal of interesting work is being done on this, for example by the Organization for Economic and Commercial Development (OECD) and the World Health Organization (WHO). One central question will be: how can we tell how well what we are doing in the UK works? It is essential that indicators are developed to permit accurate assessment of where we are now, so that sensible benchmarks can be set on where we want to be by the year 2015. This emphasis is about perpetuating the Körner cause.

We are at an inflexion point in healthcare, with advances in biomedical science, and looming developments in genetics, pharmacology, computing and nanotechnology all acting as agents for change. But our health systems are still unable to deliver a consistently high level of error-free healthcare. Data that support the development of evidence should be of proven value to individuals, the population and patients. Sound policy and IT should assist everyone concerned with the healthcare system, but above all should help clinicians to improve their operational decisions. We also need to provide consumers and patients with accurate information that stimulates them to demand action to improve the service they receive. Measurement and reporting lie at the heart of the ability to identify where errors are occurring, and the need to deal with them, as well as giving those funding the health system the ability to control and direct their resources more accurately. Empowering the public is one of the potentially largest drivers for improvement in our healthcare system. There is a degree of dissatisfaction among patients with the outcomes in the present NHS and this may be a potent means of building pressure for change. Information initiatives are important.

The role of information and IT should also be central to improving the quality of healthcare. It is already almost impossible for clinicians to keep abreast of advances in their fields, and even the present rate of advance in knowledge might soon overwhelm doctors, so it is clear that it is impossible for individual doctors to cope with the impending genetics revolution. There is a need for information and IT systems that assist doctors and patients at the point of decision. We need visionary information, information systems and communications technology projects almost akin to putting a man on the moon to achieve a goal which would not only be of immense benefit to societies in industrialised countries, but could also be of relevance in developing countries.

Lastly, I would like to focus on public interest in information. We now live in a period where public disclosure of information about quality at the level of named hospitals, doctors and primary care organisations, is becoming the norm. In the USA this movement is being driven by a variety of stakeholders – government, business and the public. In the UK, the government (with some public support) is the primary force behind the movement. At the core of this movement is the concept that producing public information about the quality of care actually provided will complement all those who are putting systems in place to improve quality. The public disclosure of information should help the quality of care improve rapidly in the first three decades in the 21st century, faster than it did in the last three decades of the 20th century. The hope is that the provision of appropriate data, information and intelligence will contribute to more rapid improvement in the delivery of quality healthcare – no overuse, underuse or misuse of medical interventions. This is the continuing Körner challenge.

John Wyn Owen CB
Secretary
Nuffield Trust
April 2003

Reference

1   Dargie C, Dawson S and Garside P (2000) *Policy Futures for UK Health. 2000 report.* Nuffield Trust, London.

CHAPTER 1

Edith Körner: visionary, NHS reformer and friend

Alastair Mason

The background

In 1975, Prime Minister Harold Wilson set up a Royal Commission to consider the best use and management of the financial and staff resources of the National Health Service (NHS). It reported in July 1979 to a Conservative government that accepted the larger part of the 117 recommendations.

As usual, implementation was dominated by structural change. The restructuring of 1982 adopted the key recommendation to abolish area health authorities (AHAs). The new structure was to comprise 14 regional health authorities (RHAs), 192 district health authorities (DHAs) and 90 separate family practitioner committees (FPCs).

Royal Commission comments about the need to strengthen local management were also instrumental in the genesis of the management review, led by Roy Griffiths, and the consequent implementation of the general management function in 1984.

The royal commissioners severely criticised the state of the national information systems, which were broadly unchanged from those existing before the previous NHS re-organisation of 1974. In particular, they were concerned about the lack of information available for monitoring and controlling resource utilisation.

The regionally organised computerised hospital activity analysis statistical system contained data about all inpatients discharged from general hospitals. From this regional database a 10% sample was submitted to the Department of Health to form the national hospital inpatient enquiry database. There was a separate mental health enquiry containing information about discharges from psychiatric hospitals and units. A variety of systems collected data about maternity events. The major managerial data sources were Form SH 3, the annual facilities return from each hospital, and Form SBH 203, containing waiting list data. These systems formed a body of statistical data for policy use by the Department of Health, from which standard summary tables were published in report form, inevitably with a time delay. There were major concerns about data accuracy and timeliness, and the relevance to contemporary clinical practice, of the definitions and classifications of all these systems.

However, the royal commissioners also identified some promising information research projects. As part of the 'clinicians in management' initiative in the late 1970s, two former district administrators, John Yates and Iden Wickings, were successfully developing new techniques for performance indicators and clinical budgeting. In 1982, concerns about deaths after operations led to the confidential enquiry into peri-operative deaths being set up. Some computing projects were beginning to show the benefits that electronic data capture and storage might bring.

It was against this background that the NHS/DHSS Steering Group on Health Services Information carried out its work from 1980 to 1985.

The steering group

The terms of reference of the steering group were as follows:

> To agree, implement and keep under review principles and procedures to guide the future development of health service information systems; to identify and resolve health service information issues requiring a co-ordinated approach; to review health service information systems; and to consider proposals for changes to, or developments in, health service information systems arising elsewhere and, if acceptable, to assess priorities for their development and implementation.

The steering group was to be permanent (to 'keep under review'), to have primacy in information matters (to 'resolve issues requiring a co-ordinated approach') and to be responsible for implementing its proposals. Mrs Edith Körner, vice-chair of the South Western Regional Health Authority, was appointed as chair.

At the time civil servants were very uncomfortable with the concept that an independent, and thus difficult to control, group should be given responsibility to implement its own recommendations. Mrs Körner took her case direct to Secretary of State, Patrick Jenkin, and obtained the implementation commitment that she wanted. The political timing was opportune because in 1980 there was emphasis on greater decentralisation of the NHS, and recognition by ministers that those in the periphery should have more influence on the centre.

Although the remit of the steering group was theoretically wide-ranging, in practice it was seriously limited by not covering primary care or IT and computer systems. The 1982 restructuring had kept the management and delivery of primary care services separate from the hospital and community services and those responsible for policy in the Department of Health and Social Security (DHSS) fought successfully to have general practice information omitted from the scutiny of the steering group. NHS computer personnel, worried about their perceived loss of power, managed to persuade the DHSS to set up a separate NHS Computer Policy Committee in 1981. Despite the original commitment in its remit to the primacy of the steering group, the Computer Policy Committee was given prime responsibility for IT, thus setting the pattern for the next 20 years, with NHS computing firmly in the hands of 'technocrats' and not users.

The steering group focused on information for health service management. Although extremely interested in all aspects of information, it did not directly consider epidemiological information about the occurrence of disease, the health needs of populations or health status. Information for clinicians to evaluate their care was not considered unless there were clinical groups willing to work with them. Sophisticated data sets were developed only for accident and emergency consultants and maternity services professionals.

Mrs Körner controlled the membership of her group tightly. Members were chosen for their expertise and experience. The only people there as representatives were consultants nominated by the Joint Consultants' Committee. NHS administrators, finance officers and information experts heavily outnumbered the few civil servants.

An innovation insisted on by Mrs Körner was that the secretariat should be chosen by her and owe its loyalty to her and not to the civil service from which it came. Indeed, in the first three months a founder member was replaced for failing to comply with this requirement. Although essential for the smooth working of the steering group, such allegiance did not necessarily advance the future careers of civil servants forming the secretariat!

Much to the consternation of the civil service, Mrs Körner insisted that all the papers of the steering group should be made available to anybody who wished to see them. The thoughts and deliberations of the group were not to be kept secret, and interested people were actively encouraged to contribute to its work.

The chair

By choosing the hitherto little-known vice-chair of the South Western RHA to become chair of the steering group, ministers cannot have imagined the force they were unleashing. Mrs Körner may not have had a reputation outside her region, but within it her ability to tackle and solve the really difficult problems without fear or favour was legendary.

I find it very difficult to write objectively about this extraordinary woman. As so many adverse things have happened to the NHS it is impossible not to look back at the early 1980s as a golden age. Memories thus tend to be rose-coloured. However, David King, one of Mrs Körner's closest NHS friends, summed up her qualities admirably in *Walk Don't Run*, the original set of essays to honour Mrs Körner, published in 1985:

> She established her authority by brute ability, being better informed and working harder than anyone else. Everyone accepts that she knows more about the subject and has read more (in several languages) about it than any two other people. Hers is not merely a detailed knowledge of a limited technical subject, for her grasp of health services internationally and the changes they are undergoing provide a general context into which the invaluable auxiliary information fits.

> Mrs Körner's commitment to the task and her capacity for hard work never flagged, even when, in addition to everything else, she was found to be rattling over every inch of British Rail's track to attend or address meetings. Happily, these formidable qualities are leavened with a keen sense of humour, and when Körner activity was in full flood, it was rare to meet anyone engaged in it who did not start the conversation with the latest anecdote or *bon mot*.

> Powerful intellect and incisive humour are not always an endearing combination unless, as in her case, they go with a genuine regard for others, whatever their station and ability. This respect and affection for the NHS and its staff were apparent to all, and people sensed that here was a reformer with her heart in the right place.

The friend

Colleagues who have suffered over the last 15 years with chairs, bent solely on supporting the political fancies of the day, will envy the relationships we had within the steering group. Mrs Körner was a Jewess, born originally in Czechoslovakia, and blessed with many of the talents of this culturally rich group of immigrants who arrived during the 1930s.

Like the archetype Jewish grandmother she worried. She worried about the progress of the work; she worried about us in the secretariat, and she worried, above all, from day one, about how recommendations were to be implemented. Indeed, Mrs Körner was only happy when she was worrying. Many a Friday evening I received a telephone call about a new danger facing us, allowing me to share it with her over the weekend. This constant concern about what was, and what might happen, underpinned an attention to detail and the rapid resolution of potential conflicts that were essential to the successful completion of the work

Mrs Körner's command of the English language was unsurpassed. Tom Stoppard, a fellow countryman, sent her his plays in draft for comment. She wrote brilliant satirical pieces for the health and social services journal, including the cult-status column 'Dear Charles'. Although we in the secretariat did the technical writing, Mrs Körner meticulously corrected the punctuation, added a final literary gloss and chose the frequently obscure but always apt quotation associated with each publication. The clarity of the writing was a major reason for the ready acceptance of the recommendations by NHS staff.

We travelled endlessly to market our proposals and to hear the views of the NHS face-to-face. However inept the comment or malicious the intent, she treated all questioners as intellectual equals and never put down or embarrassed them in public. This active engagement with NHS rank and file engendered a respect and affection still held today by all who were involved. There was feeling amongst many that although they may not have understood the technical merits of the recommendations they must be good because she was.

Mrs Körner took a genuine interest in our families, sharing concern about childhood ailments and offering excellent advice about educational and behavioural problems. One of my children in his teens needed some time and space to himself, and she and her husband, typically generous, entertained him for a week with very successful results.

Indeed, the most memorable experience of that period was a personal moment not a work one. Three years into the project we were invited to a World Health Organization (WHO) conference in Düsseldorf. This was the first time she had returned to Germany since travelling through it alone in 1938 in a sealed railway carriage as a 17-year-old girl on the way to freedom in England. Though very apprehensive she behaved with dignity and supreme professionalism. The only clue to the inner turmoil of emotions was the doubling of an already significant nicotine habit. It was a privilege to have been with her.

The vision

The work done by the steering group was informed by the clear vision developed by its chair. The activity focused on information for health service management. The guiding principle governing the approach was that data should be collected because they are essential for operational purposes. User-orientated information yields benefits to those who collect it, and thus provides an incentive for accuracy and expedition. From this simple central vision there emerged a number of logical consequences.

- The central DHSS returns, which at that time totally dominated the development of information systems, must be determined by the data required locally. The information needs of district management should be paramount and the data submitted to the DHSS confined to a small subset of the district data set.
- Every DHA and its officers need a minimum amount of data available to them, collected as a by-product of operational processes, to carry out their management function. An authority not regularly using such data is handicapped by being inadequately informed when fulfilling its responsibilities.
- The recommendations about data items to be included in the district minimum data set should be a compromise between the desirable, the feasible and the affordable. It was felt that this pragmatic approach would lead to proposals adopted in a reasonable timescale, with feasibility being defined as implementable within three years
- In order to make informed judgements about their own performance, members and officers require information not only about their own district but also comparable information about others. To enhance the validity of such comparisons, standard definitions and classifications should be developed for each requisite data item.
- Although the district minimum data set is relevant to operational managers, most units and departments will wish to collect more data for their own purposes. However, the variety of local arrangements militates against the national prescription of standard data sets for every managerial entity.
- To meet the increasing need for IT within districts, considerable design work is essential to ensure compatibility between different computer systems. Investment in computer systems was considered by the steering group to be only justified when the benefits of better information were added to the improvements in operational processes.
- As clinical and management practices change, data collected about hospital patients and resources have to be altered to accord with current reality. The minimum data set is therefore not set for all time. Its relevance must be regularly reviewed and its content appropriately updated.

Rarely can a national group reforming the NHS have had such a simple sustainable vision; one that is as relevant to today's health economies as it was to the DHAs of the 1980s.

The work

The work for which the steering group became best known was the development of the district minimum data sets. Seven working groups were set up to review the information needed to cover all aspects of heath authority activity, manpower and management accounting. To reflect the vision, the work in each area was done in two stages. Groups of NHS experts were brought together to develop the minimum data set. No civil servants, no representatives of special interest groups or external management consultants were involved. The talent was all from within the NHS.

Once the district needs had been identified, a second group (with civil servants as well as NHS staff) agreed the subset of the minimum data set that would be made available to the DHSS. All the recommended data items were defined and classified. Any new data items, definitions or classifications were piloted for feasibility of collection in four participating health districts.

Extensive consultation took place on each report. In addition to the usual formal written exercise, numerous meetings were held with specialist groups nationally and regional gatherings all over the country. An innovative feature was the setting up of Körner Klubs at four regional centres which met quarterly to be kept abreast of developments and to feed back their views and comments.

In view of subsequent events it is interesting that the only significant criticism came from computer professionals who objected not to the products but to the lack of one of their systems-based methodologies to support them. Great care was taken to ensure that the final reports showed signs of having been changed as a result of the consultation process.

Given this open process in which the NHS was totally involved, when published, the reports contained no surprises and were in tune with the needs of health authorities and their management teams. Indeed, everything was done to make implementation feel a natural extension of the development work.

It became clear at the outset that recommendations about new data would not of themselves ensure the effective provision of information for health service management. The steering group therefore embarked on a parallel programme to improve the environment in which data were collected and information produced. A working group was set up to develop standards for maintaining the confidentiality of patient and employee data. Numerous workshops of NHS experts were held to develop best practice for medical records, district information services, data standards and library services. Training materials were developed using, for the first time in the NHS, videos and computer-based interactive techniques.

Despite not having formal responsibility for computing issues, the steering group supported two important IT clinical developments. The computer-based accident and emergency records project was based in Leeds and piloted at three sites. The maternity project involved funding seven sites to develop software, all using the minimum data set.

One area that the steering group decided not to address directly was the development and specification of the information that should be presented to health authorities. It was felt very strongly that initiatives of this kind would depress the creativity of NHS managers. However, the group did commission

Christopher Day of the Health Services Management Centre at Birmingham University to write a book to help members of authorities to identify their information needs.

The publications

The steering group's publications are shown below (*see* opposite). There were seven reports to the Secretary of State. Two working group reports were published directly by the steering group. Seven occasional papers on information issues were published by the King's Fund. As a tribute to Mrs Körner, a collection of essays by key participants in the work was published in 1985.

The outcome

As the minimum data set reports came out from 1982 onwards and the moment for pressing the implementation button arrived, there was a crucial change in ministers. Out went devolver Patrick Jenkin and in came centraliser Norman Fowler.

Although ministers praised the work, there was no way they felt they could entrust the crucial task of implementation to the steering group. Mrs Körner, knowing that key civil servants did not share her vision and that they were very concerned about their loss of central control and power, insisted that the new ministers honoured the commitments of their predecessors. With an impasse of this nature there is only one outcome. Mrs Körner resigned from the steering group and the computer technocrats in the DHSS became responsible for implementation.

Without Mrs Körner the steering group limped on for another six months, completing the development work before being put out of its misery in 1985. Despite taking every conceivable precaution to ensure that the vision could be sustained she was beaten by the political process. Within a couple of years the NHS information culture had reverted. The needs of the DHSS were again paramount. The central returns, now ironically called Körner returns, multiplied and assumed ever-increasing importance.

The legacy

In the introduction to *Walk Don't Run*, Robert Maxwell, Director of the King's Fund, encapsulated the hopes of many senior NHS personnel when he wrote:

Steering group publications

Reports to the Secretary of State
- *First Report to the Secretary of State: a report on the collection and use of information about hospital clinical activity*, 1982
- *Collection and Use of Information about Transport Services*, 1984
- *Collection and Use of Information about Health Services Manpower*, 1984
- *Collection and Use of Information about Activity in Hospitals and the Community*, 1984
- *Collection and Use of Information about Services For and in the Community*, 1984
- *Collection and Use of Information about Health Services Finance*, 1984
- *Collection and Use of Information about Maternity Services*, 1985

Reports published by the steering group
- Confidentiality working group: *The Protection and Maintenance of Confidentiality of Patient and Employee Data*, 1984
- Dental working group: *The Collection and Use of Information about Dental Services*, 1985

Occasional papers published by the King's Fund
- *Converting Data into Information*, 1982
- *Introducing IT in the District Office*, 1983
- *Developing a District IT Policy*, 1983
- *Piloting Körner*, 1984
- *Making Data Credible*, 1984
- *Enabling Clinical Work*, 1985
- *Providing a District Library Service*, 1985

Books published by the King's Fund
- *Walk Don't Run*, edited by Alastair Mason and Victor Morrison, 1985
- *From Facts to Figures*, by Christopher Day, 1985

Perhaps I may make two final comments that are not directly connected with the task of implementing the Steering Group's findings. The first is a plea that the energy released by the device of a genuine partnership between the NHS and the DHSS will be remembered. It points to the advantage of challenging people at all levels in the service to take an active rather than a passive role in problem resolution. It also underlines that NHS people and DHSS people can be far more effective working closely together rather than at arm's length.

The second comment concerns the need to see the Körner reports as an important stage in the continuing evolution of health services information, not as an end point. It would show a sad unawareness of Mrs Körner's quickness and breadth of mind to allow NHS information systems to set in concrete, rather than continue to develop.

Sadly, the challenge was not forthcoming again and the concrete set. If any contemporary NHS manager thinks of Körner it is in the context of the ever more burdensome central returns and the use of the finished consultant episode as the currency of the internal market. Both perceptions are nothing to do with the work of the steering group but reflect the way that civil servants have used the Körner name to maintain their centrally determined approach to national information systems.

Mrs Körner had a powerful but simple vision that was ably communicated to, and accepted by, the NHS but was not palatable to the DHSS. A series of technically competent products about data content and the information environment spelt out the necessary detail to ensure the vision could be implemented.

All this was for naught when, in one of the periodic political swings from decentralisation to centralisation, ministers and their advisers decided that she could not be trusted to implement her proposals in a way that would be acceptable to the DHSS. Instead, they handed over this crucial task to her greatest critics. The primacy of the user was replaced by dominance of the computer technocrat, and devolved management again dominated by central demands. Unfortunately, in that process the name of the visionary driving force has been tarnished through association with an approach which breached her own clear principles.

NHS information services, and consequently all attempts at NHS reform, have suffered ever since. Moreover, the enduring lessons on effective management of innovation in information systems have continued to go unheeded.

CHAPTER 2

Learning from history

Jeannette Muphy

Introduction

It is now more than 20 years since the Department of Health and Social Security (DHSS) set up the NHS/DHSS Steering Group on Health Services Information, chaired by Edith Körner. This initiative was the first comprehensive and detailed review of the statistics available for health service management since the health service was founded in 1948.

Is there any justification now for revisiting and reassessing the achievements of Mrs Körner and her colleagues? A quick glance through the indexes of several contemporary textbooks of health informatics suggests that the current generation of health information students and practitioners is very unlikely to be exposed to the goals and methods of the steering group. At the same time, an older generation of clinicians and managers may feel that Körner's work is quite irrelevant to the challenges they face in the wake of *Information for Health*.[1] For some, the steering group may seem an anachronism, a throwback to the days before the internet, clinical codes, electronic patient records and trust intranets. If we subscribe to the view that the solution to current information problems in the NHS lies with advances in communication and information technologies then Edith Körner seems to have little relevance to the challenges facing the health service today.

The goal of this chapter is to challenge this perception by demonstrating that Mrs Körner's insight and initiative still have relevance for the NHS and to all those involved with the modernisation agenda. The reason for her continuing relevance lies in the fact that she identified a set of methodological and epistemological problems which are as relevant today as they were 20 years ago. More to the point, some of her recommendations that were not implemented are worth revisiting.

Körner's vision

I remember how astonished I was when I first encountered the six reports produced by the steering group chaired by Edith Körner from 1980 to 1984. It was

in the early 1990s (just before the launch of the first national health information strategy) and I was designing a health informatics course for health science
students. When I started to read about Mrs Körner's work, the first thing that
struck me was the scope of her project and how much she and her team had
achieved in such a brief time. In the space of four years, the steering group
looked at the collection and use of information about:

- hospital facilities and diagnostic services
- patient transport services
- health services manpower
- paramedical services and miscellaneous
- community services
- health services finance.

I was intrigued to know more about the chair – who was she; how did she come
to take on the task of reforming the way in which information was captured and
used; and what methods did she use to carry out this herculean task? But above
all, I wanted to know what motivated her to devote five years of her life to this
project. What was her vision? The first surprise when I started to investigate
was the fact that she did not come from either a 'techie' or an information
science background. Nor was she a clinician. Uniquely, Mrs Körner brought to
the job her managerial experience, a capacity for hard work and a commitment
to an open, participatory approach to the task of rethinking the information
needs of the NHS. As I read about her and the work of the steering group, I was
struck by the clarity of their vision and the revolutionary implications of what
they were seeking to achieve.

What was Edith Körner's agenda?

One quote I came across seemed to encapsulate the Körner project:

> the majority have preferred to denigrate the statistics rather than improve
> them and face the music[2]

Edith Körner was out of step with the majority; she was committed to finding a
way to improve the way that data were collected and statistics generated. But
the improvements she was seeking extended far beyond better data quality and
information systems. On the surface, it may seem that the focus of the steering
group was on number-crunching: statistics, data definitions and minimum data
sets. But in fact, from reading the reports and other documents produced by the
steering group and the working groups, it is clear that the protocols for data

collection and the statistics were just a means to an end. The real goal was to improve the quality of healthcare. Speaking at a conference in 1983, Mrs Körner said that she saw the working party as the means of reaching the true objectives of the NHS, namely better health for more people.[3]

My reading of Edith Körner's approach to reforming the system of data collection suggests that she was aware of trends in the commercial sector where chief executives were waking up to the value of information and the need to have a corporate approach to information. Under her chairmanship, the steering group adopted this concept:

> Edith Körner's review of NHS information marked a significant turning point in central returns as well as other areas of information around non-aggregated data. For the first time in an overt way the starting point was to talk about the business of the NHS and then construct the data needed to support the business functions.[4]

The steering group saw its project as being at the very heart of the changes that were taking place in the health service. It could see that political and economic pressures would bring new demands for accountability, and at the same time the introduction of new models of management was imminent. What needed to be done was 'to align the collection, processing and dissemination of information in the NHS to clinical and economic realities of the present and the future'.[5]

In this emerging climate, managers and clinicians needed better-quality data to allow them to determine:

- the population they serve
- whether the population receives the services it needs
- how those services are provided
- whether services are as good as one would like them to be.[6]

What strikes me as significant about Mrs Körner's vision of the role of health information is that it was grounded in a shrewd reading of where the world was moving and how this would impinge on public services in general and the health services in particular. But her vision was wedded to an unshakeable commitment to the core values of the NHS. Although the Körner reports are often characterised as being pragmatic, this does not mean they were devoid of ideals.

The challenge facing Mrs Körner was to convince a wide range of stakeholders that changes were needed, and to give clear guidance on how things needed to change. To appreciate the scale of this challenge we need to consider what the world was like in 1980 when the Secretary of State for Social Services set up the NHS/DHSS Steering Group on Health Services Information.

The state of health information systems in 1980

- NHS information systems had evolved in a haphazard manner over 30 years. New information systems were created in an *ad hoc* manner in response to perceived information requirements.
- There was confusion over the ownership and purpose of existing information systems.
- Different people collected rather similar information for different masters.
- Most systems of data collection were centrally imposed.
- Consequently, there were many separate systems built to provide data for the DHSS that were not used locally
- Staff on the ground were fearful of interpreting the data they collected.
- No single person or department had responsibility for making sense of data flows.
- An absence of technology meant that manual systems were used for entering data. Data entry was slow, time-consuming, labour-intensive and prone to errors.
- In regional and national centres, there were computers but these were large cumbersome, mainframe machines.[7]

Immediate drivers for change

In the decade leading up to Körner, critics of the way in which health information was gathered and used became more vocal. They pointed out that in the absence of a national information system which makes it possible to compare performance, we have not so much an NHS as a collection of local health services. The decision to commission a comprehensive review of health information services in 1980 was a response to four separate reports in the 1970s.

In 1972, the report on management arrangements noted that 'existing information is sometimes unreliable, of doubtful relevance and out of date, and there are gaps in what is available'.[8]

In 1976, the three chairman's reports noted that 'much information [was] demanded quite unnecessarily and ... that the Department and Service should jointly embark upon (a) study based upon the simple question: "Is what you are collecting of value; and who actually uses it?" '.[9]

Also in 1976, the resource allocation working party identified 'a clear and pressing need for improvement in the data routinely collected'.[10]

Lastly, in 1979 the Merrison Commission provided a very damning appraisal of NHS information: 'The information available to assist decision makers in the NHS leaves much to be desired. Relevant information may not be available at all, or in the wrong form. Information that is produced is often too late to assist decisions or may be of dubious accuracy'.[11]

To summarise, the charges were: that there was a lack of clarity about what information was needed; that data quality was suspect; that there were gaps in provision; and that there were problems with accessibility, timeliness and presentation. Clearly, there was urgent need for reform.

The terms of reference for the steering group were very broad:

- to agree, implement and keep under review principles and procedures to guide future development of health service information systems
- to identify and resolve health service information issues requiring a co-ordinated approach
- to review existing health service information systems
- to consider proposals for changes to, or development in, health service information systems arising elsewhere and, if acceptable, to assess priorities for their development and implementation.

To appreciate what Edith Körner achieved, given this broad brief and the tight timescale for delivering the reports, it is useful to look at the process by which the steering group collected its evidence, as well as some of its recommendations.

Creating the evidence base for the proposed reforms

Although the members of the steering group may have had their private views as to the best way of overhauling NHS information services, the approach they

---

Steering group working methods

1   Find out about the information requirements of a district health authority (DHA) and its management team.
2   Investigate any additional needs – of regional health authorities (RHAs) and central government departments.
3   Develop definitions and classifications for the data items that are to be collected to satisfy identified requirements.
4   Field-test the recommendations in at least four health districts.
5   Consult about the recommendations, both formally (for example, circulation of working papers and interim versions of recommendations) and informally (through a series of regional seminars).
6   Finalise recommendations in the light of field-testing and consultations; point out the likely resource consequences and a feasible timetable for implementation.

adopted to their work was very pragmatic. Reading the reports and the sup-
plementary material, it is very apparent that members of this group were not
theoreticians or academics, but people who were very connected to the realities
of the NHS. Furthermore, they were aware of the need to test their assumptions,
to find out if their proposed reforms were feasible (what we would nowadays
think of as 'rapid prototyping').

   Their working method was to build a model (such as their interim reports)
and then test in the reality of the workplace whether the ideas were feasible.
Four NHS health districts volunteered to act as test-beds for this work. From
the report of their experiences,[12] the working methods of the steering group
can be summarised (*see* box).

Whatever one might think of what the steering group achieved, it is very hard to
fault its method. If you are trying to make sense of chaos, and to engage all the
stakeholders, the Körner approach seems an eminently sensible way forward.

What did Mrs Körner achieve? How much of her vision survives?

The following are the nine elements that make up Edith Körner's vision of information management in the NHS:

1   Data would be captured as close to the patient as possible.
2   Clinicians would be more involved in data capture and have a greater sense
    of ownership of the data.
3   Only relevant, useful data would be recorded.
4   Data would be accurate and timely.
5   It would be easy to aggregate data and make comparisons.
6   Both managers and clinicians would trust the data.
7   Patients could be confident that their personal information was secure and
    protected.
8   All staff would have ongoing education and training to ensure they were
    able to both collect and use data.
9   The minimum data set would be a starting point for districts, which would
    add additional data to meet their needs.

Has this vision stood the test of time? I think that Mrs Körner's vision has proved
to be remarkably robust. Apart from queries about the scope of the minimum
data set, most of us today could still sign up to her conception of what a
well-organised information system would be like. The principles she enunciated
20 years ago mirror the rules and exhortations found in most contemporary books on the design of information systems. Her vision encompasses good

practice with respect to data quality and information capture, and also demonstrates a firm grasp of socio-organisational issues. The one element which you might say is absent from this sketch of Mrs Körner's vision is a reference to technology. This omission is quite deliberate because my reading of her suggests that she firmly believed that technology could not deliver benefits unless there is an integrated concept of the objectives of the organisation. So technology is a way of delivering the vision but it is not part of the vision.

To achieve the vision, the steering group argued that the following actions needed to be taken:

- Create an information environment in which all who work in the NHS care about data and have the education, training and support needed to work with data.
- Establish the credibility of data – ensure it is trusted, easy to access, easy to understand, and, most importantly, easy to turn into information.
- Foster a culture in the NHS in which clinicians and managers use information to inform decision, to plan for the future, to monitor performance and outcomes.

In a sense these are all actions that had to be part and parcel of the implementation phase. The thinking behind all this is that if these conditions are fulfilled, patients will benefit. Edith Körner's vision anticipated a rational NHS, where decisions were based on information, intelligence and evidence.

On what basis should we judge the Körner reports?

When trying to fill out a scorecard on the Körner report we need to decide by whose standards we should appraise the work. The analysis that follows was derived from two sets of criteria: first, a checklist of logical measures of success; second, the objectives Mrs Körner set for herself and the steering group. The verdict of her critics will be considered towards the end of this chapter.

- *Did the steering group finish the task it set out to do in the designated time?* Here, the answer is 'yes'. The steering group wound up its work in 1984 with publication of its sixth report.
- *Did the steering group use an explicit method and did it consult widely?* Full marks here. Its method is clearly spelled out and the consultative process was extensive.
- *Were the recommendations of the steering group accepted?* Yes – in April 1984 the government decided to back the national implementation of the Körner

recommendations and issued HC84(10), which set out the implementation timetable.

- *Were the recommendations of the steering group implemented?* Here the answer is both 'yes' and 'no'. Although the reports were accepted, and a deadline for implementation was set (1987), not all the recommendations were implemented.

Writing from the perspective of an IT professional, in 1986 Windsor[13] documented the missed deadlines and the fact that implementation was only partial. He cites three reasons for this:

- unreal expectations about IT
- an underestimation of the work involved
- insufficient staff training and involvement.

Leaving Windsor's caveats to one side, by and large on the basis of the four questions asked earlier, the Körner project should be judged to have been a success. But, as the steering group clearly recognised, this would be misleading:

the success or failure of our work will be judged not by the quality of our reports or by the successful implementation of our recommendations about data and systems. *The key criterion by which our performance must be assessed is the extent to which the information derived from the new data sets is used to make decisions about the allocation, planning and review of resources* [author's italics].[14]

In other words, Edith Körner set very stringent criteria by which to judge the success of her work. Did the Körner reports break the vicious cycle of underuse of information and poor quality of data collected? Here I think the answer is 'no'. To back up this assertion, there is evidence to suggest that in the post-Körner environment, the availability and use of health information did not show marked improvement.

In 1988, the Social Services Committee had this to say about the quality and usefulness of health information:

The last major weakness of the National Health Service is that it is not possible to tell whether or not it works. There are no outcome measures to speak of other than that of crude numbers of patients treated. There is little monitoring on behalf of the public. As a result, the correct level of funding for the NHS cannot be determined.[15]

Commenting about NHS information in 1992 (five years after the Körner reports were meant to have been implemented), Cyril Chantler noted that

'To outside observers the lack of relevant information for management in the NHS is surprising.'[16]

Barbara Young, writing as President of the Institute of Health Services Management, in the Foreword to *Information for Action*, also suggested that, despite the Körner reforms, managers remained disengaged from the information agenda:

> As a result of the Körner initiative, and the widespread introduction of information technology, Health Service managers now have access to more information than ever before. And yet many managers believe that they are not yet making the most of the information that is available.[17]

Further evidence that Mrs Körner failed to bring about changes in information practices can be inferred from the list of questions (*see* box) the British Medical Association (BMA), in the early 1990s, said needed to be asked about information. These questions show considerable overlap with those she posed, suggesting again that the reports had not had the desired impact.

Questions the BMA thought needed to be answered about health information

- How much information is needed?
- What information is required?
- How may it be collected most cost-effectively?
- How should it be made available and to whom?
- Where do priorities lie in funding health, administrative and management information systems?

Explaining why the NHS failed to take on board Edith Körner's vision

In trying to disentangle the various threads of what was been attempted, what was achieved and what did not succeeded, it is useful to revisit Mrs Körner's thinking at the time of the publication of the *First Report*. What we find is that from the outset Edith Körner was aware that even if the recommendations of the steering group about what data to be collected routinely were implemented, this would not ensure the effective provision of information for health service management (*First Report*, p 9).[14] Quite rightly Mrs Körner maintained that the success or failure of her work rested on bringing about cultural change in the NHS so that managers were willing to use information:

there is still, deep in the NHS management culture, a strong resistance to use even the simplest qualitative techniques.[18]

Managers give numerous excuses to justify their failure to be informed, one of the most common being that data cannot be trusted. Although Mrs Körner recognised that there was some truth to this claim, she felt it also provided an excuse for inaction. To change this situation, a whole range of measures needed to be put in place to develop an information culture, for example education and training, skills audit, development of data standards, development of best administrative practice for safeguarding patient data and promotion of the use of IT:

> We are also concerned with assisting in the creation of an environment which will allow and encourage the efficient collection, collation, processing and transmission of data.[18]

Looking back now more than 20 years since the steering group began its work, we must admit that the necessary cultural and organisational changes have still not occurred. But do we place this failure at Edith Körner's doorstep?

I think it would be most unfair to blame the steering group for having failed to promote better use of information in the NHS. Nor does the fact that Edith Körner did not succeed in achieving what she had set out to do mean the vision was flawed. To understand the fact that we are still struggling to cultivate a culture which values and uses information we need to look at what happened between the time the reports were commissioned and the time they were delivered. With hindsight, we can identify six interconnected developments which undermined Mrs Körner's agenda.

First, there were major political and economic changes; the whole landscape of the public sector changed significantly from the time Mrs Körner began her work. The phrase that is sometimes used to characterise this change is 'the end of the era of optimism'. The medical sociologist, Mary Ann Elston, describes the emergence of a new climate in which questioning the efficiency and effectiveness of medicine's use of resources became a more legitimate activity for politicians. 'The swift introduction, following the Griffiths Report in 1983, of general managers charged with responsibility for the efficient use of resources,' Elston suggests, 'apparently cut a swathe across established lines of professional responsibility and clinical freedom.'[19] 'By 1985, it was possible to identify a series of (government) moves which arguably at least are beginning to amount to a confrontation with the medical profession.'[19]

The reaction of the professions is encapsulated in Trevor Clay's pronouncement, 'The Griffiths Inquiry ... signalled the demise of professional power in the NHS. The doctors were deemed important only in so far as they could be nudged into management' (as quoted by Elston pp. 68–69).[19]

Second, in response to this demise of consensus politics, clinicians were less receptive to some of the thinking behind Edith Körner. Feeling under pressure as a result of the changes taking place in the NHS, they were mistrustful of an initiative which required them to be more open and transparent about their work and their use of resources. IT, along with information systems, were coming to be seen as a tool for being able to control doctors by providing data on cost and outcome of medical procedures.

Third, Mrs Körner was adamant that her proposals for improving information quality rested on assumptions about the competence and political will of authorities and their officers.[20] By the late 1980s, health service managers were also experiencing new pressures and were inclined to be wary about something as potentially subversive as well-presented information that allows valid comparisons. Managers, Yates argues, are frightened to explore some of the issues raised by statistical data. Information can be used both to solve problems and to identify problems.[21] Without the backing and goodwill of doctors and managers, the success of the Körner project was in jeopardy from the outset.

Fourth, the changes recommended by the Körner steering group were far more costly to implement than had been imagined. To capture the minimum data sets required investment in systems and training. To set up and manage information services new monies needed to be identified. And then, of course, there was the looming cost of computerisation. Many observers have pointed out that the necessary investment in both people and technology was not forthcoming.

Fifth, although computers were supposed to be part of the solution, in some ways they were part of the problem. The arrival of more computers, with the launch of first national Information Strategy in 1992, led to a shift in the discourse from information to technology. Willcocks and Marks maintain that given the lack of staff resources which made it difficult to meet the implementation deadlines, computerisation came to be seen as a prerequisite for achieving the Körner implementation dates.

> the NHS has been pushed from information into Information Technology to the extent the two have become synonymous, especially in general management's eyes.[22]

Edith Körner never thought the computer would be the panacea to the information problems of the NHS information. In her preface to the workshop proceedings, *Developing a District IT Policy*, she put her finger on the key problem – technology is seen as the holy grail, but for technology to deliver benefits, managers need to be understand what information systems can and cannot do. She perceived that we are in a Heraclidean landscape, with the river of technology changing from moment to moment. To survive in this situation, we need to be nimble and adaptable, 'only a process in which teaching learning and doing interact constantly with each other, will allow us to acquire and maintain the skills which we shall need in the years to come'.[23]

Mrs Körner was also percipient in her observation that the problems of applying IT solutions in a healthcare environment are not just technical, 'they extend to structural concerns of centralisation and decentralisation and to the respective roles of technical experts *vis-à-vis* lay computer users'. To rephrase this in modern jargon, Edith Körner was aware that when developing a coherent information policy and an IT system, some process re-engineering may well need to take place.

Sixth, the process of culture change was much more difficult to achieve than anticipated. Despite Körner's repeated messages about the need to invest in people, a coherent education, training and professional development strategy was not set in place. Even today we are still wrestling with the problem of how best to prepare clinicians, managers and administrative and clerical staff to value and use information. To paraphrase the American sociologist Daniel Bell, we all live in an information society; we are all information workers, but few of us are prepared to play this role.

In the final chapter of *Walk Don't Run* Yates reflects on the costs of using information.[21] His appraisal goes beyond the obvious financial costs. One of the costs Yates identifies is a willingness to change working practices on the basis of information. This, in turn, means being able to take on the vested interests that prefer to maintain the status quo. Yates hints that Edith herself paid the price of fighting to establish an 'evidence-based health care system'. He suggests that Mrs Körner was not surprised by some of the reactions to her work, 'she recognised from the outset that *spring cleaning* the NHS information system would be a mammoth task, and probably completely thankless.'

Throughout my research into Edith Körner's work, and her legacy, I have continued to puzzle over what sort of person she was. My abiding impression is that she was often misunderstood and criticised for what she did not do. Her critics seemed reluctant to give her credit for what she had attempted. I empathise with her long struggle to combat the view that a commitment to rigorous methods is somehow incompatible with humanistic values. As a teacher, I have very vivid memories of my struggle to convince nurses and social workers of the need to be numerate and computer-literate. They justified their resistance on the grounds they were 'people-focused' and they did not see why I wanted them to deal with numbers and computers. When addressing the Annual Study Conference of Health Visitors in 1983, Mrs Körner was taken to task by her audience for thinking it was possible to quantify their work. Health visitors expressed doubts as to whether the breadth and depth of what they do on a home visit could be portrayed by a statistic. Her reply was both poignant and revealing, 'Statistics', she said, 'are people with the tears wiped off.'[3]

Edith Körner was well aware that her work was far from neutral. A study of information-gathering in the NHS was potentially subversive for two reasons.

First, because it exposed poor organisational design and a lack of rigorous think-ing about the way clinical work was scheduled and delivered. Second, the crea-tion of credible data would make it more difficult for clinicians and managers to conceal poor practice. Her awareness of the political implications of her work is nicely demonstrated in the choice of quotes used at the start of the six pamphlets illuminating different phases of the work of the steering group. The quotations range from Machiavelli: *The Prince*, to John Galbraith: *The Age of Uncertainty* and John Stewart Mill: *On Liberty*.

There is little doubt that even today, after two national information strategies, there is still a gap between data collection and the intelligent use of information. Does this means that Edith Körner failed? I feel this judgement would be too harsh. The fact that she did not create an environment where all participants were able to understand their role in the information agenda can be interpreted in various ways. As suggested previously, the challenges of organisational development and providing adequate education and training for all who collect and use information were greater than anticipated. To achieve this demanded a level of investment and sustained leadership that was not forthcoming. Further-more, although there were various drivers for change, the really big seismic forces had not yet hit the NHS in the mid-1980s. Audit, risk management and clinical governance were still on the distant horizon.

Edith Körner: a beginning not an end

Many of Mrs Körner's critics have accused her of bequeathing the NHS an inflex-ible legacy, the Körner returns. Another frequently heard charge is that her minimum data sets turned into normative data sets that stifled innovation and development. The implication of these comments is that she had a very narrow concept of the information requirements of the NHS. But if we listen to her own words, it is very clear that Mrs Körner saw her work as a beginning, not an end. Writing for the *Health Service Journal* in 1987, she made clear that information systems need to be kept under review and changed as the world changes:

> The health service finds itself today at a dangerous juncture in information development. Most of the data specified as the national minimum are, or soon will be collected.[24]

At the stage she was writing (October 1987), the steering group reports had been accepted and were in the process of being implemented. But far from feel-ing that the battle had been won, Mrs Körner was all too aware of the fragility of what had been achieved 'because too many people mistake the milestone for the finishing post'.

The danger stemmed from the fact that people might not appreciate that what was needed was not a once and forever reform of information systems but a state of permanent revolution. In her words, 'It is essential that everyone concerned be made to realise and accept that we are moving towards not an event but a process'. Information management is not 'a task that can be put to bed when completed, or a routine which, once established, can be left to run by its own momentum. It is a demanding and iterative task'.[24] (Those involved in implementing *Information for Health*[1] and *Building the Information Core*[25] might consider having these words emblazoned on their doors.)

Edith Körner was particularly concerned to warn the NHS that in relation to information there were no simple cures, and that it would be a terrible mistake for her work to be reified – for the minimum data set to come to be seen as immutable and for thinking to be frozen as a result of her reports. As far as Mrs Körner was concerned the NHS information edifice was not complete and she was utterly opposed to the prospect that information strategies might be delegated to experts.

Körner saw information as a way of mapping the real world. As the world changes, so the information needed to describe it changes. Edith echoed the Greek philosopher Heraclides when she said, 'Thus, while the information task is iterative, it is not like painting the Forth Bridge: both the bridge and the method of painting change even as we are painting it.'[24]

In 1987 Mrs Körner recognised that already the data items proposed by the steering group were 'feeling the tooth of time'. 'In the five years which have elapsed since publication of the first report, the NHS world has changed sufficiently for some of our data definitions and data sets to need revision.'[24]

Appraisals of Edith Körner: diverse views of the legacy

Appraisals of Edith Körner's work fall into three distinct categories: those that see her as helping to liberate health information services; those that deplore the Körner legacy; and those that view her as a mixed blessing.

Let us start by hearing from those who applaud the Körner legacy:

On reflection, the Körner statistical revolution probably remains the single most important event in the first 50 years of NHS information and will influence thinking at the start of the new millennium. It raised the profile of information but perhaps more importantly, for the first time took a corporate rather than piecemeal look at the needs of the service, ending the separation of data for local and central requirements.[4]

The health service after Körner ... is at least a more rational system. The management and use of information within the system is better understood, defined and standardised, which must lead, particularly with the national introduction of health care computers, to better patient care.[26]

The Steering Group ... provided the basic building blocks of information for managing the health services.[27]

Mrs Körner's great contribution to the development of IT was to discern as a prime objective the production of credible information for managers and clinicians; and it is this objective that determines the technology required.[28]

The Körner reports may also be seen as a natural first step in preparing for future managerial and organisational changes in the NHS. ... both the government and Körner had such policy directions in mind when developing NHS information requirements in the early 1980s.[22]

Many of Edith Körner's critics focus on the unintended consequences of the steering group reports and recommendations, and the problems not tackled:

Körner's system is still with us, and forms the basis of the national performance indicators. These have been widely criticised – perhaps condemned is a better word – principally in the basis that they reflect *input* and *process* measures, and largely omit *outputs* and *outcomes*. Moreover, though intended for local use they reflected a centralised view of the world, and so were of limited use to those who collected them. The practical consequence for local sites was that most of their data collection efforts went on data of little local relevance and most felt they could not commit substantial extra resources to the collection of other, more relevant data.[29]

With hindsight the work by Edith Körner and her colleagues can be seen to have underpinned subsequent moves to the general management concept and then the internal market. It is unfortunate that much of their initial logic and work was seen by the DHSS as making a stick to beat the NHS with: the resultant stick was called the 'Department of Health Central Returns'.[30]

Knox and colleagues spelled out the deficiencies of the Körner reports from the perspective of community medicine. These authors took issue with the terms of reference to which the steering group worked:

The data sets delineated by the Steering Group were directed more towards managing the *institutions*, the *finances* and the *resources* of the NHS and less toward evaluating, monitoring, enhancing and managing the *function* and *effectiveness* of health- and health-care programmes.[31]

Some commentators, whilst critical of some of the consequences (largely unintended) of the Körner reports, do give her credit for her vision. Gowing, for example, sees both the negative and positive side to the Körner legacy:

> These aims were admirable and, if achieved, were to support the development of general management in the NHS. However, the real outcome was that 'implementing Körner' became an end point in itself. Whilst Körner returns may have been helpful to the Department of Health, their usefulness within health authorities, in hospitals and for doctors has been extremely questionable.[32]

> Körner did, however, ensure that information and IT were put on the management agenda ... The need for systems in turn led to resources being assigned to this area and particularly to the establishment of information and IT departments.[32]

Similarly, Windsor, at the start of his critique of Körner, pays tribute to her breadth of vision:

> There is no doubt that Körner is the most important event ever to hit management information in the NHS. Nor is there any doubt that it is, in scale, breadth and quality, a remarkable achievement. . . . Körner broke with the pattern of nearly forty years of apathy about information systems in the NHS. For the first time the corporate and not the piecemeal needs of the service have been structured: one of the reports' main achievements must be the end of the nonsense of separate data for local and central requirements. . . . Its breath of coverage is unrivalled.[13]

What is also interesting about Windsor's reflections on Mrs Körner is that he feels that, far from being disloyal in seeking to identify the flaws in the Körner recommendations, constructive criticism would help to ensure the success of the enterprise.

Unfinished business

It would be beyond the scope of the current chapter to respond to each of these criticisms. My general view is that many of the critics focus on what Edith

Körner did *not* do and ignore the cogent reasons she gives for limiting her investigation to the needs of NHS managers and her rationale for not addressing epidemiological concerns:

> The Steering Group's main concern is with information for health services management. Thus we have not tackled specifically the information needed by health professionals to evaluate the results of their care; nor that needed by individual professional bodies to review the resources to and the professional work of their members. [14]

But, as the preamble went on to say, clinicians would find much in the report to assist them when reviewing their performance and the amount of resources devoted to their activities. As for what we now call 'health needs assessment', the steering group had this to say:

> In our work we have not directly considered information about the occurrence of disease or about the health needs of populations except in so far as these can be inferred from data about hospital episodes and certain community health programmes; nor have we made recommendations about data describing health status or the clinical and social outcomes of the use of health services. [14]

Mrs Körner's justification for excluding epidemiological data was that it lay outside the scope of her work. And, regarding health status and social outcomes, ever the realist, Körner observed that:

> Methods of measuring these important variables are not sufficiently developed to allow their introduction as a routine in health service information systems. When further research has identified those indicators which are not only sought by health service managers but are also capable of routine collection in all health districts consideration will be given to their inclusion in the minimum data set. [14]

Final reflections

In any consideration of a vision for health information, the last word must be Edith Körner's. In 1984, after all the recommendations of the steering group had been accepted by the Secretary of State, Mrs Körner wrote a article for the *British Medical Journal* in which she issued a wake-up call to clinicians. She warned doctors of the big battles that were raging over resources and made it clear that they could not expect to be shielded from these. Whilst in the past such debates took place behind closed doors between the Cabinet and the

DHSS, in the years ahead this struggle for funds, she predicted, would become a familiar problem to all who work in the NHS. Edith Körner's advice was blunt: to survive you will need evidence. Guesses, unsupported opinions and anecdotal evidence will not prove effective weapons in the battle for resources. This message needs to be placed alongside Mrs Körner's earlier exhortation to doctors to improve the quality of data on diagnoses and operative procedures. She pointed out that as this data is recorded by doctors in their clinical notes, it is they who are solely responsible for the quality of this data. She was well aware of the implications of this advice and why it might be ignored. 'The procedures to maintain high levels of accuracy and completeness of these data items may impose an unwelcome discipline on doctors who record them.'[18]

In 1984 Edith Körner stood down as the chair of the steering group. She reflected on what she had achieved and the challenges that lay ahead. This was her parting message to the health service:

> The Steering Group has led the NHS to the water and cleansed it of sediment and impurities. Given the country's economic and political condition, the service will refuse to drink at its peril.[5]

References

1 NHS Executive (1998) *Information for Health*. NHS Executive, Leeds.

2 King D (1985) Mrs Körner and her Steering Group. In: A Mason and V Morrison (eds) *Walk Don't Run: a collection of essays on information issues published to honour Mrs Edith Körner CBE*. King Edward's Hospital Fund for London, London.

3 Körner E (1983) Statistics are people with the tears wiped off. *Health Visitor*. **56**: 441–2.

4 Kempner V (2000) Statistical returns: past, present and future. In: D Leadbeter (ed) *Harnessing Official Statistics*. Radcliffe Medical Press, Oxford.

5 Körner E (1984) Improving information for the NHS. *BMJ*. **289**: 1635–6.

6 Day C (1985) *From Figures to Facts*. King's Fund (on behalf of NHS/DHSS Health Services Information Steering Group), London.

7 Mason A and Morrison V (eds) (1985). *Walk Don't Run: a collection of essays on information issues published to honour Mrs Edith Körner CBE*. King Edward's Hospital Fund for London, London.

8 Department of Health and Social Security (1972). *Management Arrangements for the Reorganised National Health Service ('The Grey Book')*. HMSO, London.

9 Department of Health and Social Security (1976). *The Regional Chairmen's Enquiry into the Working of the DHSS in Relation to Regional Health Authorities*. Report (the three chairmen's report). Department of Health and Social Security, London.

10 Resource Allocation Working Party (1976) *Sharing Resources for Health in England (RAWP Report)*. HMSO, London.

11 Royal Commission on the National Health Service (Chairman Sir Alec Merrison) (1979) *Report*. Cmnd 7615. HMSO, London.

12 NHS/DHSS Health Services Information Steering Group (1983) *Piloting Körner: the views of senior administrators from the four districts who piloted the interim reports of working groups A to E from 1981 to 1983*. King's Fund, London.

13 Windsor P (1986) *Introducing Körner: a critical guide to the work and recommendations of the Steering Group on Health Services Information*. British Journal of Healthcare Computing Publications, Weybridge.

14 Steering Group on Health Services Information (1982) *First Report to the Secretary of State: a report on the collection and use of information about hospital clinical activity in the National Health Service*. HMSO, London.

15 Coulter A (1991) Evaluating the outcomes of health care. In: J Gabe, M Calnan and M Bury (eds) *The Sociology of the Health Service*. Routledge, London.

16 Chantler C (1992) Management and information, in the future of health care: articles published in the *British Medical Journal*, BMJ, London. **304**: 632–5.

17 Lattimer B and Mason A (no date) *Information for Action*. Institute of Health Services Management, London.

18 NHS/DHSS Health Services Information Steering Group (1984) *Making Data Credible*. King's Fund, London.

19 Elston MA (1991) The politics of professional power. In: J Gabe, M Calnan and M Bury (eds) *The Sociology of the Health Service*. Routledge, London.

20 NHS/DHSS Health Services Information Steering Group (1982) *Converting Data into Information*. King's Fund, London.

21 Yates J (1985) Using Information. In: A Mason and V Morrison (eds) *Walk Don't Run: a collection of essays on information issues published to honour Mrs Edith Körner CBE*. King Edward's Hospital Fund for London, London.

22 Willcock LP and Mark AL (1988) *Information for Management? A review of progress on information technology and general management in the UK National Health Service*. Working Paper No 92, City University Business School, London.

23 NHS/DHSS Health Services Information Steering Group (1983) *Developing a District IT Policy*. King's Fund, London.

24 Körner E (1987) Too important for the experts. *Health Service Journal*. **29 Oct**: 1258–60.

25 Department of Health. *Building the Information Core* . Department of Health, London.

26 Strickland-Hodge B, Allan B and Livesey B (1988) *Information Technology and Health Care*. Gower, Aldershot.

27 Scrivens E (1985) *Policy, Power and Information Technology in the National Health Service*. (Bath Social Policy Paper No. 3) University of Bath, Bath.

28 Peel V (1995) Information management and technology strategy for healthcare organisations. In: R Sheaff and V Peel (eds) *Managing Health Service Information Systems: an introduction.* Open University Press, Buckingham.

29 Keen J (1994) Information policy in the National Health Service. In: J Keen (ed.) *Information Management in Health Services.* Open University Press, Buckingham.

30 Nicholson L and Peel V (1995) Manpower development for NHS information systems. In: R Sheaff and V Peel (eds) *Managing Health Service Information Systems: an introduction.* Open University Press, Buckingham.

31 Knox EG (1987) *Health-Care Information.* Nuffield Provincial Hospitals Trust, London.

32 Gowing W (1994) Operational systems. In: J Keen (ed.) (1994) *Information Management in Health Services.* Open University Press, Buckingham.

CHAPTER 3

Improving the United Kingdom's health system: an adaptive model to harness information and evidence

Don E Detmer

Introduction

These are stressful times for the healthcare sectors of all nations, and the United Kingdom is no exception.[1-6] Health system shortcomings are widely publicised, funding remains tight, public expectations for improved performance are growing, and many people want more direct involvement in their own care. New knowledge and technologies create an abundance of opportunities to improve health, but inadequate diffusion mechanisms or limited resources often hinder their impact. Healthcare in the near future must continue to deliver acute, episodic care to individuals (the old business) and simultaneously provide much better chronic illness management for both individuals and populations (a newer business). The challenge for all nations is to redesign their complex care systems.[7,8] Neither a straight top-down nor a bottom-up approach will work; rather, change must occur throughout systems over time.

Despite a strong commitment from health professionals to improve health, their effectiveness is determined largely by the system in which they operate. A healthcare system is only as good as the skills and ideas of its people, the processes and infrastructure they use to accomplish their work, and the culture that supports their efforts. Today each of these critical components is distressed and only the adoption of a clear longer-range strategy will truly integrate efforts and lead to a modernised service. Considerable effort is already being devoted to identifying the kinds of changes needed and how best to implement them. It is timely and appropriate to identify the critical leverage points for transformation of the health system.

The times call for vision and leadership – a vision simple enough to carry in one's head and leadership that both motivates reluctant souls to respond to relevant messages and allows the experimentation needed for changes to occur. A strong vision that is effectively communicated by leaders and eventually embraced by the broader health community is not, however, sufficient to reach the objective of a transformed health system for the 21st century. Leaders must assure that organisational systems are both flexible and sufficiently aligned with stated goals. They must support a culture whose values drive them toward needed actions. Further, the vision that will shape the evolution of the health system must be constantly refined to accommodate the ever-growing base of knowledge on what constitutes effective health services. There needs to be a permanent means of ensuring that the vision stays ahead of the system and that the system's development is generally consistent with the vision and available evidence. And, a proper knowledge and information technology infrastructure (what Canadians call an 'infostructure') must underpin it all.[9]

The four recommendations presented here create an integrated regimen for improving performance of the United Kingdom's health systems. The first recommendation calls for a national academy of health to provide continuous visible-thought leadership for the health system that can withstand and channel the winds of open political discourse and media hype. The second recommendation calls for a set of principles to guide reform efforts. The third recommendation develops informed leadership through a clinical scholars' programme and a corresponding redesign of the work setting to provide prepared clinician-executives with the time, authority and resources needed to perform their leadership roles. The fourth recommendation establishes an information and knowledge platform as essential to improving the organisation and delivery of care. These recommendations will complement the recent set of policy initiatives by the Department of Health and the other home countries' health departments, and enhance performance of whatever system emerges from the current reform debate in the United Kingdom.

Recommendation 1: establish a national, independent body to guide health policy development

This politicization of technical debates about health policy greatly impedes – one might say, prevents – an informed, calm, public debate about the future of the health care system.

RGA Feachem

One of the major impediments to true transformation for the NHS is the degree to which the NHS is exposed to political winds and expected to respond to the latest public concern. The UK lacks a representative group of health experts to bring sufficiently broad and seasoned input to the table to contemplate and create new and more acceptably framed programmes for change that are not linked to any particular political party. The current situation needs to be replaced by a steady, evidence-based course of action that builds on past experiences and policies so that there is a long-term sense of policy direction and better continuity for policy that influences individuals working within the NHS.

A Royal (National) Academy of Health (R/NAH) would provide needed authority, independence and credibility for UK health policy and NHS strategy development. The R/NAH would be a membership organisation modelled on the Institute of Medicine (IOM) in the USA (as described below). It would be broadly representative of the health professions and include distinguished individuals of related disciplines who are willing to volunteer their relevant expertise to critical health issues facing the nation, much like the Foresight Programme or the Academy of Medical Sciences, but with all relevant disciplines represented. The new organisation would provide guidance to the governments on critical health policy questions while remaining independent of immediate political demands. The primary role of the R/NAH would be to provide unequivocal evidence derived from analysis, synthesis and constructive deliberation. Reliance on scientific rigor and consensus development would provide crucial ballast against shifting political winds and a buffer against an incessant media that is interested in 'human interest' for hype and sales as much as constructive social change. In addition to producing useful, evidence-based reports, the R/NAH would also provide a mechanism for creating more mature informed leaders.

The R/NAH would respond to specific policy questions (for example, what are the implications of wait times on health status; when are wait times acceptable and when are they detrimental; is this policy generally functional or dysfunctional?), would help to define the health agenda for the UK (such as, which of the myriad white papers and reports should form the basis for action; what are the most important tasks for health system reform; what should the transformation platform look like?) and articulate policy in terms of action steps for a variety of stakeholders. Further, the R/NAH would play an important role in educating the public on the complexity of health policy issues.

The IOM was established in 1970 as a non-profit organisation that is a branch of the National Academy of Sciences. Its mission is to 'advance and disseminate scientific knowledge to improve human health'.[10] The IOM strives to 'obtain the most authoritative, objective, and scientifically balanced answers to difficult questions of national importance'. It provides information and advice concerning health and science policy to government, the corporate sector, the professions and the public through its studies and reports. The federal government requests and funds the majority of IOM studies but committees of volunteer scientists selected totally by the IOM processes conduct the actual studies. The IOM carefully composes these committees to assure the necessary expertise, and to mitigate complicating bias or conflict of interest. The committee reports undergo extensive review and evaluation for scientific merit and rigorous evidence by a group of relevant experts who remain anonymous until the study is published.

The IOM also organises round tables, workshops and symposia to provide an opportunity for public and private sector experts to 'openly discuss contentious issues in an environment that promotes evidence-based dialogue'. The IOM also manages the Robert Wood Johnson Health Policy Fellowship Program, designed to develop the capacity of outstanding mid-career health professionals in academic and community-based settings to assume leadership roles in health policy and management. (In time, such a programme would be a useful adjunct to the clinical scholars' initiatives discussed below.)

In addition, the IOM is an honorific membership organisation. Members are elected on the basis of their professional achievements and serve without compensation in studies and other activities on health policy issues. One-quarter of members must be selected from professions other than those primarily concerned with medicine and health; members are represented from natural, social and behavioural sciences, law, administration and engineering. This mixture is crucial since it creates a rich pool of experts to allow panels to be created on a wide variety of studies. Foreign members add greatly to the quality of deliberations. Non-members are also invited to participate in study committees to ensure balanced representation of views and the highest calibre of technical expertise. The IOM works through a set of boards composed of members and staffed by the IOM. The board structure assures that work is done across a number of relevant topic domains that include children, youth and families, food and nutrition, global health, healthcare services, health promotion and disease prevention, health sciences policy, cancer policy, neuroscience and behavioural health, and health policy programmes and fellowships.

Over its 30-year history, IOM studies have addressed a wide variety of issues ranging from disparities in healthcare among races and ethnic groups to biological threats and terrorism, from improving palliative care for cancer to family violence.[11–14] The IOM special initiative on healthcare quality resulted in two pivotal reports on patient safety and healthcare quality that provided a call to action and a framework for achieving threshold improvements in safety and quality.[2,3] These reports, *To Err is Human* and *Crossing the Quality Chasm*, have received some attention in the UK. The quality initiative is ongoing and now has a major IT component as well to address specific policy issues raised in those reports, such as identification of priority areas for quality improvement, outlining a national healthcare quality report, guiding development of patient safety data standards and creating a robust national information infrastructure. These reports and national events led the US Secretary of Health and Human

Services to request a study to offer the government advice on next steps. This report, *Fostering Rapid Advances in Health Care: learning from system demonstrations*, outlines a set of major statewide initiatives to create the seeds for the future US healthcare system.[15] It has received a strongly positive response from the media in the USA.

In the area of IT and information policy alone, the IOM and the National Research Council of the National Academy of Sciences have produced a series of reports that have brought important health information technology issues to the attention of the federal government. Indeed, they helped put these issues on the national agenda. These reports include:

- *The Computer-based Patient Record: an essential technology for health care*[16,17]
- *Health Data in the Information Age: use disclosure and privacy*[18]
- *Telemedicine: a guide for assessing telecommunications in health care*[19]
- *For the Record: protecting electronic health information*[20]
- *Trust in Cyberspace*[21]
- *Networking Health: prescriptions for the internet*[22]

Two important recent reports from the US government:

- *Transforming Health Care Through Information Technology* (President's Information Technology Advisory Committee, 2001)[23]
- *Information for Health: a strategy for building the national health information infrastructure* (National Committee on Vital and Health Statistics, 2001)[24]

drew heavily from the conclusions and recommendations of the IOM and NRC reports and the individuals who had been part of the studies.

Recommendation 2: adopt a finite set of simple rules to guide major change

The maxims of complex adaptive systems (CAS) offer new insights on how to achieve profound change within a dynamic environment and are replacing the command and control models for organisation and change management.[25] The science of CAS recognises that many systems, including healthcare, are not fully predictable. Not only can the elements of CAS change themselves, but creativity is also a natural part of any complex system. As a result, it is difficult to predict how a CAS will behave. Yet despite these considerations, a CAS can be orderly without central control. A few simple rules applied locally can yield complex outcomes (for example, maintenance of a huge colony of insects or the Internet).

A fundamental lesson from CAS for the reformulation of the health system is to provide a 'good enough' vision along with a set of simple rules, and then to allow generous latitude for innovation. Without any rules, complex systems will experience chaos rather than progress because there are too many possible paths to follow. With a set of rules or values to guide thinking and action, multiple small changes throughout complex systems can result in major improvements over time through a 'biological' kind of evolution. Immediate change is not the goal. Rather, one seeks to use simple rules and minimum specifications so that gradually changes evolve from the natural creativity of actors making improvements throughout the system. In time less adaptive processes are then dropped in an evolutionary fashion. When one is uncertain about what to do in either building a component of a new system or approaching a patient, one can examine the potential choices for action against the basic rules.

There is a distinct need for clarity. Participants in the system need to be able to discern the rules easily. The blizzard of new policy initiatives and visions, and targets and 'reform' directives emanating from Whitehall over the past few years would be sufficient to confuse any group of leaders as well as potential followers. Further, too many rules limit flexibility and innovation, and thwart constructive incremental change.

What then constitutes the 'good enough' vision and what kind of rules are needed to guide the redesign of the health system? The IOM has provided these pivotal elements and more for the US healthcare sector in its report, *Crossing the Quality Chasm: a new health system for the 21st century*.[3] The IOM vision comprises two components – a statement of purpose and a set of six aims for the system.

> *Purpose*: The purpose of the healthcare system is 'to continually reduce the burden of illness, injury, and disability, and to improve the health and functioning of the people' of the nation (p. 6).

> *Aims*: '. . . [C]are must be delivered by systems that are carefully and consciously designed to provide care that is safe, effective, patient-centered, timely, efficient, and equitable' (p. 7).[3]

Health professionals and decision-makers can easily remember the purpose and aims since they are clear and basic and they share tacit validity. Despite their simplicity, they are comprehensive and relevant for all health systems.

Certainly, one wishes to have care that is *safe*. The precept of doing no harm while seeking to help the patient is an ancient one. An ethical system of care should not waste resources on care whose benefits are unproven, hence *effectiveness* is important. Further, if one pursues effectiveness wherever it may lead, significant changes in care systems may well develop over time. Care, defined as health services, may possibly change one day into more effective community education policies. *Patient-centred care* is subtle and can be a challenge to focus upon since one can rather easily say that virtually everything is there to some extent to focus on the patient. What is intended is to have, to the maximal extent possible, patients at the centre of their care with respect to decisions, responsibility, and style and manner of delivery. This has not been a design feature of many of our care processes. This becomes even more important as chronic illness becomes a more dominant component of illness patterns (World Health Organization, 2001).[26]

Care should be *timely*. Some problems can be safely put aside, whereas good care in other instances must be prompt care to be any care at all. As the old adage goes, 'a stitch in time saves nine'. A care system must have a way to determine what can wait and what cannot wait and triage patients accordingly. *Efficient* care is important since there are always insufficient resources and wastefulness is essentially care that is not given to someone else who might benefit from it. Lastly, care should be *equitable*. Obviously, there may be times when these criteria come into conflict but much of the time they do not.

To achieve the six aims, healthcare organisations need to redesign their systems. According to the IOM, healthcare process redesign should be based as well on 10 principles (*see* box). Health professionals need to be supported in their efforts to implement these redesign rules. The health system must offer appropriate training opportunities and incentives that encourage behaviour consistent with the rules. Information systems will play a critical role in putting these rules into routine practice (*see* rule 4 below).

Redesign rules for healthcare processes[3]

1 Care is based on continuous healing relationships
2 Care is customised according to patients' needs and values
3 The patient is the source of control
4 Knowledge is shared and information flows freely
5 Decision-making is evidence-based
6 Safety is a system priority
7 Transparency is necessary for patients and their families to make informed decisions
8 Needs are anticipated
9 Waste is continuously reduced
10 Co-operation among clinicians is a priority

Recommendation 3: strengthen leadership throughout the health system through educational opportunities and restructured roles within their work settings

Effective leaders move their organisations or communities from vision to reality, idea to action and the abstract to the concrete.[27] The transformation process entails four basic steps. First, leaders must be able to convince their constituents of the need for change and motivate them to act by describing their vision and delineating goals, often in the form of stories. Second, leaders must enable and encourage the organisation to succeed by building the platform (skills, tools and incentives) that will enable and encourage change. Third, the members of the organisation must act. Fourth, the organisation, including its leaders, must learn from successes and mistakes to improve its performance.

The nature of leadership has changed in recent years to accommodate changes in organisational structure, culture and practices. Effective leaders are more likely to be found throughout organisations and society, to share information and power, and to possess both strong technical expertise and 'emotional intelligence'.[28] The leadership needed to initiate and support dramatic change will not appear *deus ex machina*. It must be cultivated by organisations, and future leaders need opportunities to refine their skills.

Further, there is a need for both organisations and individuals to understand the distinction between being a manager and being a leader. Managers are important for smooth operations while leaders determine future directions for their organisation or unit. Leaders set the tone for their organisation through their communications, behaviours and the goals they set for the organisation, its personnel and themselves. It is particularly important that leaders understand the various constituencies that are part of their organisation so that they can translate their message to suit different audiences.

Leaders assume that their managers and staff are proficient in three critical information skills – finding and using evidence to guide clinical and administrative decisions, using data to generate new knowledge and evidence, and redesigning clinical and administrative processes. Success in the new health system will depend on a leader's ability to foster collaboration and cross-fertilisation among different disciplines and across organisational lines. Leaders must be externally focused and play a critical role in forging organisational relationships that will enhance its ability to succeed. Lastly, leaders must be willing to make decisions, take risks, act on their decisions and learn from both their successes and failures.

The NHS has a serious problem in the knowledge and skill base of its most crucial group of change agents. Its highly respected clinical leaders are competent in their clinical disciplines but those who are tagged to become leaders or who have the instincts and capabilities for being first-rate medical or nursing directors or leads on a variety of new programmes move into these posts with a minimum of appropriate academic preparation. It is no surprise that many people in such positions do not give the job adequate attention and think it is less important than the clinical backlogs they also face. Yet it is the innovative thinking of these individuals that is needed to lead the system redesign that will help to reduce these backlogs.

Developing leadership skills is not a quick process and two-day workshops are not adequate to prepare rising leaders of the NHS. The Leadership Centre within the NHS Modernisation Agency is an important step towards addressing current shortcomings.[29] Its offerings need to be strengthened, however, through the creation of a clinical scholars' degree programme that is aimed at fostering a broad perspective and strengthening analytical skills of its participants. Only one or two first rank programmes would be required to meet the needs for the entire UK and Europe. Moreover, the resources needed to do the job properly are such that only one site in the UK will be likely to generate sufficient funding to do the job right.

The model programme would include learners pursuing master's degrees, some studying at the doctoral level, and some studying simply to gain skills and knowledge in one particular area. Those learners enrolled for the master's level courses could take them either as modular courses to meet the degree requirements or simply as continuing education courses. However, by being part of an organised curriculum, their courses would comprise a rigorous, comprehensive set of knowledge and skills needed to excel at the role of clinical leader. Approximately one-half of the curriculum would be from the core curriculum for a Master of Business Administration (MBA) degree; one-fifth would be on healthcare systems and clinical informatics; one-fifth would be focused on quality and safety; one-fifth would contain elements from a Doctor of Public Health curriculum; and the balance would be electives particularly suited to helping learners to improve their current work environment and the problems it faces. Academic faculty and an appropriate worksite 'faculty member' would collaborate in shaping simultaneously a scholarly and practical effort to address a current problem facing the organisation and then solve it. This will assure that the programme actually delivers relevant knowledge and theory while also developing the learners' practice skills. The learning goal is not knowledge *per se* but useful knowledge, including the skills to create and manage change.

A high priority of the programme is a multidisciplinary character, with both the teachers and learners being from various backgrounds and disciplines. Much of the current discontinuity in the present system exists because participants do not see themselves as members of teams where the role of each is known and is highly valued. Those who leave the programme will have changed their perspectives and sense of values. They will be more prepared to face tough issues and help those with more focused responsibilities and skills to create effective solutions combining both human resources development and relevant communication and information systems. The practicum – the practical component – will also tend to keep learners committed to their current practice setting while it builds a tradition of supporting the growth and development of talented younger people within a variety of settings (for example, primary care, community resources, hospitals). It scarcely serves the system to have people constantly shifting from one locale to another with the lost productivity such moves entail.

Those few individuals who pursue doctoral-level training will become the generation of health services researchers and leaders who help to ensure that top-quality research is pursued and that top-level health policy meets the quality standards needed for progress in healthcare systems. These people will serve as mentors and colleagues to rising generations of health professionals. Their training will have made them international in their outlook so that the advances from elsewhere are fed into the system.

In addition to a robust educational programme to develop clinical scholarship and leadership, clinical leadership roles within the NHS must be redesigned to allow those with the knowledge and skills to reinvent their environments and its systems. Achieving dramatic progress with respect to IT in the UK will involve the skills of strategic assessment and implementation as much as knowledge of information hardware and software. The chief information officer needs to be seated at the board level but only if he or she has the knowledge and skills needed to offer strategic and tactical direction.

Consider the model of how our cells work. There is important information sent from the nucleus in the form of messenger RNA to ribosomes. The ribosome is one-half nucleus and one-half cytoplasmic in its orientation. Having an intimate knowledge of both the centre and the periphery, it can create proteins (that is, policies and procedures) that are specific to cellular needs so that the cell can adapt to changing circumstances and still remain healthy. After a set of clinical scholars begin to populate the work settings as capable 'ribosomes', they must be given the materials (substrates) they need to revise, reform and create more appropriate structures, systems and modes of communication so that meaningful acceptable change can be accomplished without intense angst or strain. Indeed, much of this will eventually become 'second nature' since it basically is an organic approach used by complex adaptive systems as a way of sense-making.

The poor opinion of management and leadership within the ranks of many health professionals would suggest that an explicit programme be developed to raise the visibility and acceptability of these crucial functions. This can involve little more than acknowledging to the inside and regional community when the efforts of a team and its leader have led to clear improvements in care. Publicly acknowledging genuinely good deeds is a time-honoured way of giving a sense of acceptability to traditionally less rewarded activities.

Recommendation 4: build the information and knowledge platform that will enable practitioners to translate the envisioned health system into practice

What practices and behaviours can we expect to see in the new health system? All decisions within the health system – whether a clinical decision for an individual patient or a decision to fund a particular treatment for the entire system – will be increasingly based on evidence rather than opinion. Quality improvement will be a routine part of healthcare practice rather than an adjunct activity. Every health service organisation will become a laboratory in a sense and strive to learn from its successful and unsuccessful new pilot projects as well as newly examined routines. Integration of services and collaboration among health professionals, a range of organisations and with patients and patient groups will be the norm. Citizens will assume greater responsibility for and play a major collaborative role in managing their own health challenges. Healthcare professionals and organisations will view the determinants of health broadly and pay greater attention to the health of populations.[30]

Robust information and knowledge management capabilities will support virtually every interaction in the health system and will be pivotal to successful transformation of the health system. IT and knowledge management are critical enablers of the system redesign rules developed by the IOM (*see* box on p. 37). Citizens and patients can use information technology to develop both personal and intergenerational health histories, identify risk factors and communicate with health professionals. Facile access to reliable knowledge resources will help citizens to determine when they need to contact a health professional and aid them as they participate in decisions about treatment. Increasingly, technology is making it possible for patients with chronic disease (for example, diabetes) to monitor their health status at home while still maintaining contact with health professionals.[31]

IT is the means by which health organisations and professionals can assure that they are providing quality care to individual patients. Computer-based patient records make it possible to build complete health histories across time and across settings of care. Decision support systems bring the latest evidence to clinicians at the point and time of care. Automation of routine tasks (for example, physician order entry) reduces the potential for human error. For example, a computerised physician order entry system with drug allergy and drug–drug interaction warnings reduced non-missed dose medication errors by 80%.[32] Electronic mail offers a convenient means of maintaining contact with patients and strengthening the relationship between patients and professionals.

IT is also the means by which health organisations and professionals can improve the quality of health services for the population as a whole by strengthening the body of evidence on which health decisions are based. A system worth its salt will actively seek evidence of clinical impact in a manner that allows conclusions to be drawn based upon experience. In a managed information environment, when problems are identified that meet criteria for care, and there is sound evidence on how to obtain excellent results, one follows decision support rules so that performance does not slip and slide along in an uncertain manner. Clinicians can choose to override the decision support system when selecting among care options. However, the data on all patients is tracked over time so health professionals and system managers can review both the quality of the protocol and the impact of their decisions to override it. They can either revise the protocol to become more robust or revise their thinking and behaviour.

The decision support system is 'adapted' over time based upon the relevant evidence, both distant and local, to assure better processes of care and better outcomes. The emerging term for such decision support systems for clinical environments is 'evidence adaptive clinical decision-support systems'.[33] The hallmark of these systems will be their ability to provide the most current literature-based evidence and local practice-based evidence to clinicians. Getting 'just-in-time' knowledge that is needed at the 'point-of-decision' to make sound decisions is a role for the 'infostructure'. The architecture for the information infrastructure must be able to draw upon personal health records, patient health records and population health records as needed.[24] Only with proper design will the system allow such data to be assembled and studied so that leaders at different levels of the system can ask relevant questions and receive timely answers.

The cycle described above presumes the existence of robust and formal knowledge management capabilities within organisations and across the health sector as a whole. Information and knowledge management system developers and users need to understand that information systems are in reality echoes of face-to-face conversations or other relevant communications. The goal is to both enhance communications in the first instance and also bring to later decisions the value that was derived from earlier investigations and conversations. Further, the benefits of IT can only accrue if the information that is being transmitted or used for analysis is of high quality, if the people using the information are skilled in its application, and organisational processes are modified to take advantage of improved access to information and incorporate lessons learned from analysis of the information.

Developing a robust 'infostructure' in and of itself represents a formidable, but important and achievable challenge for each nation seeking to improve health system performance. In the UK (as in other countries), there is a crying need for greater central leadership to be taken with respect to system architecture, standards development, and movement to the internet. The appointment of the Director General of NHS Information Technology is a strongly positive move in this direction. At late-2002, the UK is literally desperate for such help, and crucial progress made at the grassroots over the past decade is likely to become more and more local in its outlook and functionalities if stronger direction is not offered from the centre. Patients, health professionals and system managers must all acquire and continue to refine their skills to use emerging information systems effectively.

Conclusion

Well done is better than well said.

Benjamin Franklin

The UK and the USA are both grappling with how to overcome the shortcomings of their current healthcare systems. They are striving to improve their approaches to rationing while dramatically improving the quality of their health services and, in so doing, ultimately improve the health status of their populations. The complexity of the endeavour should not be underestimated. Clear vision, sufficient resources and countless hours of effort must be combined with patience and creativity to transform the respective health systems. The importance of these efforts cannot be overstated, improving the health of individuals and populations always has been and always will be one of the noblest tasks for professionals and one of the most important functions of government.

Responsibility for building the 21st century health system does not lie with 'them'. It falls to each citizen, each patient, each health professional, each health system executive, each policy analyst and each legislator to do a bit more than their fair share. Citizens and patients have a responsibility to pursue healthy lifestyles and to participate actively in decisions about their healthcare. Health professionals have a responsibility to collaborate with their peers and with patients, to grow as professionals, and to embrace the forthcoming changes. Policy-makers and legislators have the responsibility for providing needed tools and adequate resources. System executives have the responsibility for helping their staff see the possibilities of a 21st century health system and encouraging experimentation that will yield new practices.

To achieve the greatest benefit from available resources, we must all be evidence-based in our decision-making and align our actions with the rules of the new health system. IT is the means by which evidence can be systematically developed, disseminated and applied throughout the system. Sound information systems combined with practices based on evidence will provide a strong foundation for the future health system and for healthier and happier lives.

References

1 Feachem RGA (2000) The future of the NHS: confronting the big questions. *Health Affairs* **19**: 128–9.

2 Institute of Medicine (2000) *To Err is Human: building a safer health system.* National Academy Press, Washington DC.

3 Institute of Medicine (2001) *Crossing the Quality Chasm: a new health system for the 21st century.* National Academy Press, Washington DC.

4 Klein R (1999) Why Britain is reorganizing its National Health Service – yet again. *Health Affairs* **17**: 111–25.

5 Smith PC (2002) Performance management in British health care: will it deliver?. *Health Affairs* **21**: 103–15.

6 Smith R (2002) Oh, NHS, thou art sick. *BMJ* **324**: 127–8.

7 King's Fund (2002) *The Future of the NHS. A Framework for Debate.* King's Fund, London.

8 Wanless D (2002) *Securing Our Future Health: taking a long-term view.* April. HM Treasury, London.

9 Office of Health and the Information Highway (2002) *Canadian Health Infostructure (CHI): introduction.* (www.hc-sc.gc.ca/ohih-bsi/chi_ics/index_e.html)

10 Institute of Medicine (2001) *Informing the Future: critical issues in health.* (www.iom.edu)

11 Institute of Medicine (2001) *Improving Palliative Care for Cancer.* National Academy Press, Washington DC.

12 Institute of Medicine (2002) *Unequal Treatment: confronting racial and ethnic disparities in health care.* National Academy Press, Washington DC.

13 Institute of Medicine (2002) *Biological Threats and Terrorism: assessing the science and response capabilities.* National Academy Press, Washington DC.

14 Institute of Medicine (2002) *Confronting Chronic Neglect: the education and training of health professionals on family violence.* National Academy Press, Washington DC.

15 Institute of Medicine (2002) *Fostering Rapid Advances in Health Care: learning from system demonstrations.* National Academy Press, Washington DC.

16 Institute of Medicine (1991) *The Computer-based Patient Record: an essential technology for health care.* RS Dick and EB Steen (eds). National Academy Press, Washington DC.

17 Institute of Medicine (1997) *The Computer-based Patient Record: an essential technology for health care.* (rev. edn.) RS Dick, EB Steen and DE Detmer (eds). National Academy Press, Washington DC.

18 Institute of Medicine (1994) *Health Data in the Information Age: use, disclosure, and privacy.* MS Donaldson and KN Lohr (eds). National Academy Press, Washington DC.

19 Institute of Medicine (1996) *Telemedicine: a guide to assessing telecommunications in health care.* MJ Field (ed). National Academy Press, Washington DC.

20 National Research Council (NRC) (1997) *For the Record: protecting electronic health information.* National Academy Press, Washington DC.

21 National Research Council (1999) *Trust in Cyberspace.* FB Schneider (ed). National Academy Press, Washington DC.

22 National Research Council (2000) *Networking Health: prescriptions for the internet.* National Academy Press, Washington DC.

23 President's Information Technology Advisory Committee (PITAC) (2001) *Transforming Health Care through Information Technology.* (www.ccic.gov/pubs/pitac.index.html)

24 National Committee on Vital and Health Statistics (2001) *Information for Health: a strategy for building the national health information infrastructure.* United States Department of Health and Human Services, Washington DC.

25 Plesk P (2001) Redesigning health care with insights from the science of complex adaptive systems. In: Institute of Medicine *Crossing the Quality Chasm: a new health system for the 21st century.* National Academy Press, Washington DC.

26 World Health Organization (2001) *Informal Meeting on Innovative Care for Chronic Condition.* (ICCC) 30–31 May. Geneva, World Health Organization.

27 Couto RA (2002) *To Give Their Gifts: community, health, and democracy.* Vanderbilt University Press, Nashville, Tennessee.

28 Goleman D (1998) *Working with Emotional Intelligence.* Bantam Books, New York.

29 NHS Modernisation Agency (2002) *Leadership Development.* (www.modernnhs.uk)

30 Blue Ridge Academic Health Group (1998) *Promoting Value and Expanded Coverage: good health is good business.* Cap Gemini Ernst & Young, Washington DC.

31 Shea S, Starren J, Weinstock RW *et al.* (2002) Columbia University's Informatics for Diabetes and Telemedicine (IDEATel) Project. *Journal of the American Medical Informatics Association* **9**: 49–55.

32 Bates DW, Teich JM, Lee J *et al.* (1999) The impact of computerized physician order entry on medication error prevention. *Journal of the American Medical Informatics Association* **6**: 313–21.

33 Sim I, Gorman P, Greenes RA *et al.* (2001) Clinical decision support systems for the practice of evidence-based medicine. *Journal of the American Medical Informatics Association* **8**: 299–308.

CHAPTER 4

The need for a new healthcare paradigm: patient-centred and knowledge-driven

JA Muir Gray and Harry Rutter

Introduction

Never has healthcare been so effective, or so criticised. About three of the five extra years of life that people have gained in the last half-century are due to the effects of progress in healthcare.[1] The developments, many of which we now take for granted, have been astonishing, ranging from renal transplantation to the treatment of migraine. However, those who provide and pay for healthcare face continuing problems as the need and demand for healthcare increases inexorably owing to population ageing, technological development and rising expectations. In almost every country the rate of increase of need and demand is greater than the rate at which additional resources can be made available by the state.

For these reasons healthcare systems always fail to meet both need and demand, leading to increased pressure for more resources. This is resisted in many countries because of the high proportion of the wealth of societies already invested in healthcare. The gap between public expectations and the reality of service delivery also leads to demands for ever higher standards of management of those resources that are available, and managerial ingenuity has been invested in the development of better systems for managing human resources, for funding healthcare, for motivating clinicians, and in new methods of organising and delivering healthcare.

One reason for our continuing problems is that we are not moving quickly enough to the new paradigm described in *The NHS Plan* and related documents, such as *An Organisation with a Memory*[2] and *The Expert Patient*,[3] described by the Chief Executive of the NHS at the South East Region conference on *Information for Health* in June 2001. The difference in emphasis between the old and the new paradigms is set out in Table 4.1.

Table 4.1 The old and the new knowledge paradigms

20th century paradigm	21st century paradigm
Professional control and responsibility	Shared control and responsibility
Single professions	Teams
Expertise	Accountability
Institutions	Networks
Services	Systems
Paper	Digital
Finance as key constraint	Knowledge and people as key constraint
Quantity	Quality and safety
Averages	Inequalities
Strategy	Delivery
Science	Humanity
Centred on professionals	Centred on patients

The response of the Department of Health to the Kennedy Report[4] on paediatric heart surgery, *Learning from Bristol*, emphasises the need to move to the new paradigm.

Many changes are needed to bring about the new paradigm. One of the most important of these is the need to realise the potential value of information and knowledge for patients, clinicians, managers and commissioners. The new paradigm has the following characteristics:

- it assumes the patient is competent and responsible
- it creates an electronic patient record as the hub of the system
- it integrates every type of document to provide a single source
- it supports clinical decision-making by delivering knowledge when and where and how it is needed
- it uses knowledge to drive quality improvement
- it allows changes in policy to be immediately communicated and implemented
- it facilitates systems and networks
- it offers research opportunities to clinicians and patients.

Coping with the explosion of knowledge

More than two million research reports are published every year. Vast amounts of data are collected about patients. Huge numbers of people work in healthcare, each of whom has expertise and experience that is rarely made explicit;

it is thus *tacit* knowledge. Patients also have a large amount of tacit knowledge that can be made explicit and useful. However, the potential usefulness of this knowledge is not fully realised because it is not managed well enough. Healthcare organisations manage money, human resources and their buildings with care and responsibility, but knowledge is not managed to this standard. Librarians manage the knowledge that is sent to libraries, but much important knowledge is not sent to libraries – knowledge about health service use and outcomes, for example. Furthermore, few libraries are properly used in supporting board decisions because board members often do not see the need to use the knowledge and skills contained in libraries for management decision-making. The internet changes all aspects of knowledge management from research to publishing and from distribution to implementation, but few health services are realising the potential that the new paradigm offers.

Knowledge management problems

Although healthcare depends on capital assets, such as buildings, it is an excellent example of a knowledge economy, namely one that is based on knowledge as an asset and in which the main products – better clinical decision-making and better treatment – depend on the effective management of knowledge. Furthermore, healthcare has it own huge research infrastructure producing knowledge specifically for the healthcare industry.

However, as a knowledge economy healthcare is cavalier about the way in which it manages knowledge, and a number of weaknesses in its knowledge management are easily observable, notably:

- poor co-ordination of knowledge sources
- poor control of knowledge flows into organisations
- poor control of knowledge flows within organisations
- poor document management
- wide variation in the knowledge available to key professionals
- failure to get new knowledge quickly and consistently into practice
- haphazard and low quality control over the knowledge produced by healthcare organisations, for example knowledge for patients.

The magnitude of these problems is immense; for example, half of all medication errors are knowledge-based, and poor document management is overloading practitioners with information: almost 23 kg of paper guidelines had been sent to all 30 000 general practitioners in the eight years to 1998.[5]

All of these problems can be tackled by more effective knowledge management.

Aims and objectives of knowledge management

The aim of knowledge management is to help individuals and organisations to achieve their objectives more efficiently through the generation, organisation, mobilisation and utilisation of knowledge. The specific objectives of knowledge management are to:

- identify the knowledge needs of each professional, patient and organisation
- develop the necessary culture, systems and structure within organisations
- ensure that the knowledge required is produced
- provide answers to questions
- convert tacit knowledge into explicit forms
- deliver knowledge when and where and how it is needed
- develop the knowledge management skills of individuals
- manage documents effectively and efficiently
- create opportunities for learning.

Improving the three dimensions of knowledge management

To improve knowledge management three inter-linked initiatives are required (Figure 4.1).

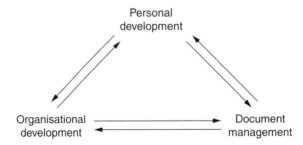

Figure 4.1   Three inter-linked initiatives to improve knowledge management.

Personal development

Although healthcare is based on knowledge and uses large amounts of resources, it is an activity delivered by people for people, and personal development is of central importance in improving knowledge management.

The level of performance of individuals within an organisation is a function of three variables: it is directly related to their competence and motivation, and inversely related to the barriers that they have to overcome. A personal development strategy therefore has to address all three of these issues (Figure 4.2).

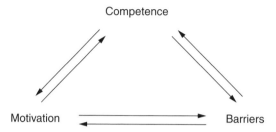

Figure 4.2 Three issues to be addressed in a personal development strategy.

Professionals and patients are highly motivated to manage knowledge to best effect but they face significant barriers in doing so, such as difficulties getting hold of knowledge. However, even with these barriers removed individuals may not have the skills that are required to:

- structure questions to make best use of knowledge
- find the relevant knowledge
- appraise the quality of the knowledge found
- tailor the knowledge to take into account the needs and values of the individual patient or population
- communicate and implement the knowledge.

Fortunately, there are now resources available to help professionals acquire or improve these skills, such as the Critical Appraisal Skills Programme (CASP) based in Oxford.

Organisational development

Three aspects of an organisation impinge upon the ability of organisations to manage knowledge culture, systems and structure (Figure 4.3).

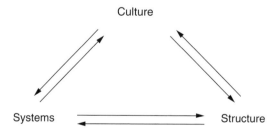

Figure 4.3 Three aspects of organisations that impinge upon their ability to manage knowledge.

Organisational change has hitherto focused primarily on structural reorganisation. But, structural reorganisation will never produce a perfect organisation for an activity as complex as healthcare. Transformation through cultural change and new knowledge management systems provides better opportunities for tackling the ubiquitous seven healthcare problems (*see* box) and maximising the value from the resources invested in healthcare. Some structural change is sometimes required, for example someone at board level needs to be identified as the Chief Knowledge Officer, analogous to a Chief Finance Officer. But the main changes that need to take place are in culture and systems.

The ubiquitous seven healthcare problems

- Clinical errors
- Unknowing variations in policy and practice
- Failure to get knowledge into practice
- Overenthusiastic adoption of new technology of low value
- Poor clinical quality
- Poor patient experience
- Waste

Document management

The term 'knowledge' is sometimes interpreted as meaning evidence derived from research, but this is only one meaning and it is too narrow. A second

Table 4.2 Document types and the knowledge they contain

Document type	Example of embedded knowledge
Policy	General principles to guide prioritisation and resource allocation
Knowledge	Information derived from data, experience or research, tailored for decision-making
Quality	How services should be provided to achieve explicit standards
Patients	Data about individual patients
Administration	Information used to organise services
Returns	Data provided for performance monitoring
Education	Resources to increase knowledge and skills
Research	Data collection questions

approach is to distinguish *tacit* knowledge, which is within the head of the person who has developed or acquired it, from *explicit* knowledge that has been written down and published. Fortunately, tacit knowledge can usually be converted into explicit knowledge without too much difficulty. Thus, people other than those who have met and spoken to the holder of the tacit knowledge can also use the knowledge that has been acquired from experience. Perhaps the simplest way to define the different types of knowledge is to classify knowledge by the objectives for which it has been prepared. Table 4.2 lists the different types of document used in healthcare.

To improve document management it is necessary to clarify which types of content will be required for particular decisions, professionals or organisations, and then, using web-based systems, to organise those documents in a way which maximises their:

- accessibility – the ease with which a document can be found, moved or stored
- usability – the ease with which it can be used for the purpose intended
- functionality – the ease with which the documents and their systems interact with all other information systems, such as the electronic patient record.

Improving knowledge management

To improve knowledge management a two-stage process is necessary in which each of these three dimensions – professional development, organisational development and document management – is analysed and then changed to improve effectiveness and efficiency.

The adoption of these new healthcare paradigms offers a different way of organising healthcare compared with the patient-centred traditional model that is based on discrete organisations such as hospitals or primary care. General moves to strengthen the infrastructure, such as increased access to broadband, are also essential, but the development and implementation of new medical knowledge paradigms offers a number of benefits, notably:

- the opportunity to interest and motivate many clinicians who are interested in reducing clinical errors, but who would be uninterested in, or cynical about, concepts such as knowledge management
- improvements in quality management
- support for national programmes of disease control by providing a knowledge framework on which better control of epilepsy or asthma could be built.

Change can be facilitated and promoted through the use of concepts, but it is essential to complement these with structural and systems measures to transform healthcare organisations from those in which knowledge plays only a minor and peripheral part in the life of the organisation to those in which knowledge is managed as carefully as money or human resources.

The knowledge system built for the Rapid Access Chest Pain Clinic web folder[6] is an example of a knowledge system that incorporates many of the features listed above and which will incorporate all the characteristics listed earlier.

Building knowledge into quality improvement

Knowledge is derived not only from research and experience. Routinely collected data produce knowledge; the Public Health Observatory is an excellent example of good knowledge management. We need to link all types of knowledge to the most important task of the NHS – looking after patients and populations, and continually improving quality and safety to improve health (Figure 4.4).

The new paradigm for healthcare could be created by, and would be driven by, well-managed knowledge.

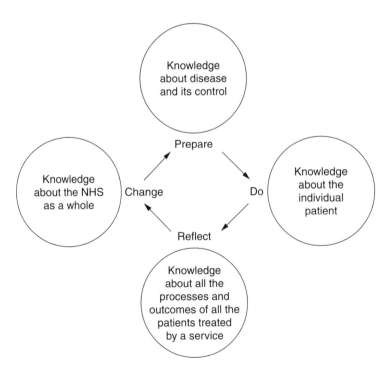

Figure 4.4   Knowledge tasks in the NHS.

References

1 Bunker J (2001) *Medicine Matters after All*. The Nuffield Trust, London.

2 Department of Health (2000) *An Organisation with a Memory*. The Stationery Office, London.

3 Department of Health (2001) *The Expert Patient: a new approach to chronic disease management for the 21st Century*. The Stationery Office, London.

4 Department of Health (2002) *Learning from Bristol: the Department of Health's response to the report of the public inquiry into children's heart surgery at the Bristol Royal Infirmary 1984–1995*. The Stationery Office, London.

5 Hibble A, Kanka D, Pencheon D *et al.* (1998) Guidelines in general practice: the new tower of Babel? *BMJ* **317**: 862–3.

6 National Electronic Library for Health Rapid Access Chest Pain Clinic project. (www.nelh.nhs.uk/heart/racpcs/dataset/racpc_intro.htm)

CHAPTER 5

Information as the patient's advocate

Michael Rigby

Introduction

Traditionally, the medical record has been an essential information store capturing the patient's history of diagnosis and treatment with a healthcare provider. By reference to this record subsequent clinicians can scan the patient's previous health experiences, but more importantly can assess the possible causes of new morbidity, and previous patterns of response to treatments, as the record speaks for the patient in a way more technically eloquent than patients themselves could achieve. Medical and nursing practice has considered the record as something which belonged to the organisation and was there for the benefit of clinicians, whereas modern thinking is that it should be considered far more as being a representation of the patient's interest.

Now, modern technology and the opportunity to interlink records give this advocacy function much greater power and wider recognition. There are also sub-groups of patients who are not able to represent themselves easily in healthcare encounters – these include: infants; patients who are comatose confused or distressed; and under some circumstances, those with a mental illness or intellectual disability. Thus as organisational concepts such as care planning become more focal to the healthcare process, so the patient's case for benefiting from a share of available healthcare resources becomes dependent upon the strength of the representation of their need as encapsulated in the record. This is additional to the traditional indirect but important function of epidemiology and public health in taking a statistical representation of a defined group of people and promoting their interests through public health measures, including identification of resource needs.

Whilst some aspects of this representation approach are rooted in history, the work of the Steering Group on Health Services Information, led by Edith Körner, represented a major step forward. In particular, the minimum data set (specified according to local functional need) is a concept that ensures comparability of representation. Some subsequent initiatives have sought to facilitate this representational role. However, as with so many initiatives that Mrs Körner's work instigated, the follow-through has been poorly focused and has not captured the imagination or striven for the goals that are desirable.

Development of record-keeping

Over the years record-keeping has been seen as a fundamental and essential part of clinical practice – for doctors, for midwives, for nurses and for other professionals. As a result, in recognition of the vital importance of the contribution of an accurate historic record to the care of the individual, professional bodies have established principles and professional standards for this task. For the individual clinician failure to study the record before treatment is perceived as reckless risk-taking (except in emergencies when the record is not available and life is at immediate risk), and concomitantly the keeping of accurate records is seen as an essential professional requirement, failure to comply with which is a disciplinary matter. In the more complex world of hospitals, with a large range of diagnostic and other information, and tremendous demands upon the records library function, a distinct medical records profession has become established, together with principles and techniques.

However, these principles and practices have emerged from centuries of keeping of paper records, largely completed by hand or more recently machine printout, and perforce restricted to the individual healthcare organisation. The record for individual patients could be held within the controlled environment of the treatment location, and thereby also linked to the particular health problems being treated there.

Given these physical constructs, communication between different treatment locations was by means of letter. Although the message would be about an individual patient – a request for a diagnostic procedure, a request for treatment for a purported condition or a discharge notification with summation of the action taken and recommendations for onward care – the views expressed were clinical interpretations. They were messages from one health professional or team to another, expressing views about the patient, and asking another clinician to undertake specific action. Although these messages concern a patient, the views are those of health professionals, and the specific wishes of the patient may or may not be strongly articulated within them.

This is a 'message in a cleft stick' approach to clinical communications, and the health records for patients begin to acquire a collection of the messages received. A particular provider's record for a patient thus extends to being a representation of the diagnosis and treatment of that patient by that health organisation, supplemented by a series of distilled views through this collection of messages from elsewhere.

Electronic opportunity, electronic challenge

This organisational messaging approach to record-keeping was the best that could be achieved in a paper-based era, but that started to change in the last quarter of the twentieth century. The advent of modern telecommunications led to widespread parts of industry and commerce dispensing with paper and relying upon electronic media for both transmission and storage of information. In many cases this passed through interim phases, such as use of facsimile machines to transmit a letter instantaneously (though with the input and output still being paper-based), but it soon migrated to full, electronic inter-connectivity. In order to bring some semblance of order to this world, standard messaging protocols became a key issue, and health organisations both within individual country health systems and internationally became involved in developing standard clinical messages. Pathology and other areas of strongly numerate clinical data, which were amenable to structuring yet where accuracy of detail was essential, led in this field. Less straightforward in the first instance were the standards to convey word-based or narrative-based information.

However, the concept of greater inter-connectivity frightened healthcare practice almost as much as it enthused industry and commerce. For instance, retail banking underwent a revolution as it grasped not just electronic recording but consumer-focused electronic interactivity. The era of customers going to a bank during set working hours, to fill in a form in order to get some of their own money put into their hand, was swept away with the advent of automatic teller machines (ATMs) available 24 hours per day and in locations convenient to consumers, who no longer needed to conform with the provider organisation's working practices in order to obtain their own money. This progressed to creating a wider range of banking services and stimulated a consumer-led refocusing of financial services. Banks had to change radically, and their structure and staffing adjusted to support consumer needs. Less conspicuously but equally significant, manufacturing organisations interlinked their operational systems, so that supplies of materials and components were ordered electronically as needed, and the whole transportation industry transformed to logistic support and just-in-time (JIT) deliveries.[1]

The health sector response to these opportunities was pedestrian. Some diagnostic departments moved rapidly to computerisation and electronic media because these significantly enhanced their patterns of working. Slowly there were moves to forms of electronic record-keeping, but these were initially very much focused upon patient registration, patient administration and business transactions. The opportunity to re-engineer the organisation and the processes was but a gentle breeze blowing against the historic temple of organisational structure and its long-established ritual procedures.

Of bright lights and mirrors, and deeper shadows

However, as the use of electronic data processing and recording crept slowly into healthcare, so some pioneers saw the light which beckoned towards greater benefits than merely the electronic automation of messaging. The work which captured the imagination was that of the US Academy of Sciences Institute of Medicine in 1991, which reached the public as a seminal volume.[2] This highlighted the benefits to the patient of information about them being held in any treatment location and being available in real time to clinicians at a later date in a totally different treatment location and regardless of the health problem being addressed.

Although the work rapidly fired the imagination, its limitations were not widely noticed. There was the lack of any costing, and no modelling of the volume of transactions and thus the electronic demands that would be made, but more significant was the fact that the means of representation of patients between healthcare organisations and locations was to be totally changed – letters and other inter-personal communication were out, and direct access to the record was in. So instead of the remote clinician initiating a person-to-person communication between health professionals that summed up the previous history or health issue, the record written by a previous clinician itself now spoke directly for the patient – it was now the patient's advocate. It spoke of the patient's wider healthcare history, with their consent (if operated appropriately), but without their needing to be present to tell the story. This was a new and unremarked attitude, whereby the record itself was assumed to be able to represent patients' full interests without clinician intervention or interpretation.

The Institute of Medicine report highlighted, appropriately, the benefits of much wider and immediate access to essential information. But inevitably it assumed that the information was largely scientific and biophysical. Underneath, the vision was built largely on the unexplored assumption that health professionals thought along similar lines, recorded by use of the same notations and used language in similar ways. And it gave little thought to how records in different settings interpreted patients' views, feelings, preferences or their life circumstances specific to their (often not fully described) personal and social contexts. It assumed a common inter-organisational language of care that had barely begun to be developed.[3]

In a healthcare world in which 10% of morbidity relates to mental illness (in its broadest definition), where family and social support is seen as a normal requirement but is intensely personalised, and where a high proportion of adults have some form of caring or supporting responsibility, this simple approach to indicating health activity with electronically held records is bound to be regressive towards the medicalisation of healthcare. Representation of patients becomes unduly focused on their biological history and previous healthcare interventions. Representation of patients' personalities and daily circumstances, the impact on daily life of functional limitations of health problems, and their aspirations and priorities for treatment outcomes, which hitherto came through the clinician-to-clinician message (where even then it was likely to be under-represented) rather than from the formal records, were now at risk of further downgrading.

Recognising the wider role of the record

One of the key issues in moving to a modern information environment in healthcare is to recognise that the traditional format of the medical record – a sequential chronology or history with some additional noting of external material – has been a necessity of limited technology, not a framework of first choice. One of the earlier proponents of a more structured approach, even in a paper-based era, came from Laurence Weed in America, who introduced the concept of the Problem Orientated Medical Record (POMR).[4,5] This sought the drawing together of patients' complaints into a structured series of problems rather than clinical phenomena, so that a more integrated or holistic approach could be taken. Concomitant with this was the use of the systematic 'SOAP' approach of seeking Subjective data then Objective data, Assessing the problem and then Planning management of the case.[6]

This, in turn, led to a focus on the planning of care. Broadly speaking, care planning was developed within nursing care to recognise that a range of activities need to be undertaken regularly, at pre-planned times, but above all for expressed purposes and with intended outcomes, and that the nursing resource should be available to meet these needs.[7] This manifests in one form in inpatient care, but the same principles apply to domiciliary care for either physical or mental conditions, where it is important that procedures are undertaken at the right time and place. In more integrated form and by various other therapy-specific titles, such as care protocols and care pathways, care planning is now a recognised approach. Indeed, it is seen as important that patients are fully aware of their care plan.

However, this is only the first move towards advocacy for patients, through ensuring that future resource requirements are recorded and thus patients' interests protected. This might be seen as resource requirement representation, rather than full advocacy. And even then, apart from specific intensive settings such as theatre rostering and acute hospital dependency-based nurse rostering, there are few examples of patients' care plans directly fuelling a health resource management function in a way that modern commercial functions would see as essential good management and service, based on customer orders or daily sales.[1]

The latent need – the true record advocacy that remains to be understood or achieved – is the further development of the record so that it truly acts on behalf of patients as their advocate under a range of different circumstances. This is particularly important bearing in mind that patients are seldom present when decisions are made that affect their treatment – decisions such as scheduling of admissions, deployment of resources or in the longer term the development of health services. And, in a range of not uncommon situations, although patients are present they are not able to represent their own interests fully at that time.

Advocacy roles of the record

Looking forward to the opportunities that ought to be created with the introduction of electronic records, and the virtual electronic record created by wider networks, there is now a new opportunity for records to act positively as patients' advocates, representing their needs in a way that cannot be overlooked. The following types of advocacy through the patient record can be considered.

Advocacy for treatment

A patient presenting and not fully able to explain themselves through reasons of illness or confusion, as well as patients being considered at a case conference, should be capable of representation from a record which presents not just their clinical symptoms but that also represents them as human beings in a social context, with personal needs and views. Thus their preferences, their responsibilities and the support available to them are equally important. Some proponents of networked electronic records in mental health have advocated these solutions and the results and benefits.[8,9] In a human values-based service, recognition of patients' preferences and beliefs should also be important, and should move from the current largely negative approach of not undertaking treatments to which patients will object, to a more positive one of recognising how patients would prefer to be treated.[10]

Resource advocacy

Healthcare resources are always overstretched, and even in the best-planned circles illness of staff or other adverse events will always disturb the pre-planned schedule and require immediate decisions. Care may be delayed, rescheduled, reduced or cancelled. In these circumstances patients are only represented by their records or their scheduled requirements.

Delivery pattern advocacy

Whilst many aspects of clinical priority are self-evident, others are lost by a simple listing of clinical procedures – for instance, rescheduling an activity to a date when a patient has a clashing commitment is likely to waste resources. An integrated or inter-linked record with details of all planned care can avoid this.

Protection advocacy

Possibly the least-appreciated of all, the record can act to protect patients. A strong yet under-realised example is in child protection, where abused children are usually presented to different health facilities in different locations so as to disguise the pattern of induced illness or injury. Subsequent studies have shown all too frequently that all the relevant information is available, but is locked into separate unlinked record systems.[11] A means of pooling, within an ethical framework, of this otherwise comparatively insignificant information in order to build up a big picture would have a protective effect. By presenting the pattern of previous presentations and problems to a health or social care professional, the record would speak on behalf of the child.

Prevention advocacy

This is more widely understood, and is based on the emergence of public health and epidemiological principles. Illness in individuals will be treated on an individual basis, but if summaries of that information are pooled then epidemiological pictures build up. Action can then be taken to address the course of a problem and to prevent further recurrence. The beneficiary of this form of population advocacy is not the group of patients who have already suffered, but their peers in the social group who are protected from also joining them. The social group itself may not have any visible cohesion. The traditional example is the identification of the Broad Street pump as a source of cholera, but in modern times possibly the least-cohesive group was people who had walked down a particular London street, who thereby contracted Legionnaire's disease. An extensive public health investigation identified the source as being a building's air conditioning system, and its elimination protected the general population.

Requirements for record advocacy

Realisation of the advocacy referral of the electronic record requires three things. First, electronic records need to be available in a locality, and with sufficient coverage of use to speak for all those in a particular category of need, or service beneficiaries. Although the core concept may have arisen from the concept of the computerised patient record,[2] it is wider, community-based networking that has made the foundations available through comprehensive coverage.[12] This broad concept is now becoming more widely enshrined in national policy, as with the initial NHS policy document, *Information for Health*.[13]

Second, as already indicated, there is considerable risk that on their own electronic records become increasingly biophysical in detail, and reduce the representation of patients' personal viewpoints and needs. Thus it is very important that electronic records contain adequate information about needs, properties and preferences, so that they truly represent patients as individuals. In order to do this appropriate elements are needed in the record structure,[9] but recorded in a sensitive yet objective way.[3]

Third, such systems need to represent the real world in terms of availability of appropriate services, practical operational arrangements to manage their deployment and general usage by the full range of healthcare professionals and first-line managers.[14,15] This needs a number of concepts to be developed and applied to healthcare that may be commonplace in other commercial services, but not so in this more complex world. These include the management of resource slots and better planning of treatment patterns, and avoidance of bottlenecks and overcommitment. Concerning topics such as the need to protect vulnerable children, the most effective balance between confidentiality and sharing key indicators of risk has yet to be achieved within the networked record system.

Conclusion

As with so many developments in healthcare, there is a risk that the development of electronic patient record systems will be driven by issues of provider organisation efficiency, and modelled largely on the apparently more expensive areas of acute care. However, as is also often the case, this will fail to look at the yield of human benefits that could and should be available by a more reflective and consumer-orientated approach. Streamlining post-operative care, for example, should be beneficial to patients and organisations. However, avoiding missed appointments in mental health or long-term support of the frail and elderly, or rapid adjustment of planned support because of a change in the patient's circumstances, will reduce the risk of adverse incidents whose human and economic costs can be even more severe. Quantifying the benefits of reducing the number of children at risk of inadequate care may be difficult, but there are clearly gains on all fronts if these problems are reduced. But even beyond these more emotional benefits, there are clearly significant gains to patients and services if the ongoing delivery of care and provision of support is more finely tuned to human facets, and if necessary short-term changes to deployment caused by staff sickness or other factors can minimise disadvantages to patients.

Moreover, the issues are not restricted merely to the immediate ones. The NHS is concerned about comparatively poor patient compliance both with delivery mechanisms, such as keeping to appointment times, and with compliance with treatment regimes. It is often not appreciated that this is exacerbated by the apparently impersonal and somewhat mechanistic structure of the service delivery system. If healthcare delivery based on modern record systems is seen to be much more people-specific and sensitive, it is more likely to increase respect for the service and thus compliance with it.

In addition, management should increasingly be evidence-based, and the necessary evidence derives in a large part from local information.[16] Wherever possible, management information should be drawn from operational systems, to minimise cost whilst valuing accuracy and timeliness. Electronic patient records are an ideal source of such data. But if operational and strategic decisions are going to be made based on the information in patients' records, it is also essential to ensure that they act effectively as patients' advocates.

In order to achieve this the focus of the record needs to move from solely that of a treatment history and a treatment booking system to one that, in all respects, speaks for and on behalf of patients in a much more personal way as an advocate. In a significant way Mrs Körner's work laid a simple foundation, by indicating the importance of the minimum data set to ensure that adequate information was recorded and shared for each patient. This was a very simple, and in the more modern technological context simplistic, approach. Nevertheless, when building upon the concept of a core set of essential data representing patients, and building into that ideas of representing patients' interests in a wider humanitarian sense, can be seen the foundations of a new paradigm of representation of patient interest in the record. Now that there is a policy drive to further speed up the implementation of electronic patient records, there is the danger that history will repeat itself and the NHS will opt for the simplest solution simply because it will be the quickest. But as we learnt from that era of short-term expediency, the core purpose will be significantly undermined. The challenge in the modern implementation of electronic information and records systems in health must be to build in the wider interests of patients, using appropriate representations through modern information concepts, so that the new record structures truly represent patients as people, and promote their interests and advocate their positions in articulate, sensitive and caring ways.

References

1   Roberts R, Rigby M and Birch K (2000) Telematics in healthcare: new paradigm, new issues. In: M Rigby, R Roberts and M Thick (eds) *Taking Health Telematics into the 21st Century*. Radcliffe Medical Press, Oxford.

2   Institute of Medicine (1991) *The Computer-Based Patient Record – an essential technology for health care*. RS Dick and EB Steen (eds) National Academy Press, Washington DC.

3   Swayne J (1993) A common language of healthcare? *Journal of Interprofessional Care* 7: 29–35.

4   Weed L (1968) Medical records that guide and teach. *NEJM* **278**: 593–600, 652–7.

5   Weed LL (1969) *Medical Records, Medical Education, and Patient Care: the problem orientated record as a basic tool*. Case Western Reserve University, Cleveland OH.

6   Savage P (2001) Problem Orientated Medical Records. *BMJ* **322**: 275–6.

7   Binnie A *et al.* (1984) *A Systematic Approach to Nursing Care – An Introduction*. Open University Press, Milton Keynes.

8   Robins SC and Rigby MJ (1995) Electronic health records as a key to objective health care needs assessment beyond the hospital boundary. In: RA Greenes, HE Peterson and DJ Protti. *Medinfo '95 – Proceedings of the Eighth World Congress on Medical Informatics, Vancouver, 23–27 July 1995*. Healthcare Computing & Communications Canada Inc., Alberta.

9   Rigby MJ and Robins SC (1996) Building healthcare delivery systems, management and information around the human facets. In: J Brender, JP Christensen and J-P Scherrer *et al.* (eds) *Medical Informatics Europe '96 – human facets in information technologies*. IOS Press, Amsterdam.

10 Rigby M (1994) Patient-focused hospitals or person-focused healthcare? *Health Services Review*, X: 8–10.

11 Noyes P (1991) *Child Abuse – a study of inquiry reports 1980–1989*. HMSO, London.

12 Rigby MJ and Nolder D (1994) Lessons from a child health system on opportunities and threats to quality from networked record systems. In: F Roger-France, J Noothoven van Goor and K Staehr-Johansen (eds) *Case-based Telematic Systems Towards Equity in Health Care* (studies in Health Technology and Informatics Vol. 14). IOS Press, Amsterdam.

13 NHS Executive (1998) *Information for Health.* Department of Health, London.

14 Rigby M and Robins S (1995) Practical success of an electronic patient record system in community care: a manifestation of the vision and discussion of the issues. In: J Runnenberg J (ed) *The Future of Patient Records – care for records for care* (Proceedings of the 8th European Health Records Conference, 21–24 May 1995, Maastricht). Dutch Association for Medical Records Administration, Hoorn.

15 Robins SC and Rigby MJ (1995) Opportunities for community services provided by integrated electronic patient records and critical success factors for achieving this in practice. In: J van der Lei and and WPA Beckers. *AMICE 95 Proceedings – Strategic Alliances between Patient Documentation and Medical Informatics.* VMBI (Dutch Society for Medical Informatics), Amsterdam.

16 Bullas S and Ariotti D (2002) *Information for Managing Healthcare Resources* (Harnessing Health Information Series No. 6). Radcliffe Medical Press, Oxford.

CHAPTER 6

Information for practice improvement

John G Williams

Introduction

In an ideal world, clinicians delivering care to the highest possible standards will be fully informed about the patients who are the subjects of their care. They will have immediate access to current evidence-based wisdom as to what is the best route to diagnosis and cure or alleviation of the condition presented. They will also know details of all the resources, facilities and expertise available to support them in achieving this, and how to access these quickly and appropriately. Clinicians will have knowledge and insight into the extent and limitations of their own expertise, and will be able to monitor their own performance regularly. Lastly, they will be able to plan and implement sensible changes to their own and their teams' practice, based on knowledge of demand, and the success and weaknesses of the service.

Patients are the prime source of information about themselves, but recall and accuracy deteriorate rapidly with time, and probably the only truly reliable information from the rational patient will describe current problems and complaints. The primary purpose of the patient record is to document details of history and care that will be of use in the immediate or long-term future. Present record systems fail to meet this primary purpose,[1] for many reasons. Most records are paper-based, and are thus often not available, particularly if needed in more than one place at a time. Paper records grow larger, and they deteriorate. Each provider organisation and professional group has its own system. Surprisingly, in hospitals there is no statutory requirement governing the structure or content of medical records, and diversity and lack of structure or organisation are commonplace. The current concept of the patient record, as a provider, speciality- and episode-based journal, is also flawed, preventing the easy generation of a clear longitudinal picture of patients' illness or health.

The ideal world envisages a simple means of capturing and storing data about patients, yielding information that is immediately available when needed, and presentable in a variety of forms, appropriate to the context of care. It is believed that electronic capture of data in both structured and free text form will enable this,[2] but the technical, cultural and organisational problems of achieving this are formidable. From the technical point of view, a generic approach to electronic clinical system development has long been advocated,[3] but progress is inhibited by short-term, speciality-specific requirements. It is being further slowed by the need to monitor the implementation of condition-focused national service frameworks that are generating their own, condition-specific data sets and data collection processes.[4,5]

The clinician's perspective

From the clinician's perspective, one of the most difficult changes in the move towards electronic records will be the development of the cognitive agility and skills needed to organise and document clinical facts to a level of detail and accuracy that has hitherto been uncommon.[6] It will mean adherence to a common language of health,[7] agreed and understood by all professionals, and including common headings for the organisation of the record.[8] There will also need to be an integration of professional perspectives, and a process for extraction of summary facts of importance for future care. Compartmentalisation by sectors of care will also have to disappear, so that an overall picture of the health and social care history and needs of the patient is obtained. Needless to say this raises important issues of confidentiality and security of information, which are further inhibiting progress.[9] It is to be hoped that theoretical constraints will be tempered with reality in the future.[10]

In an era of long overdue and increasing patient empowerment,[11] a change in culture that gives greater recognition to patients' information needs, and their wishes and preferences with regard to treatment, needs to be supported by an appropriate technical and information infrastructure. This must ensure that patients' views and preferences are made known to those who look after them, especially during times when patients may not be capable of expressing them. Similarly, the impact of care needs to be addressed more rigorously, by use of fully validated patient-focused outcome measures that are routinely collected and monitored during their care.[12]

Clinicians need information to ensure that they are up to date, delivering clinical management that is proven by research to be effective, or if this evidence is not available, equates with the consensus view of experts in the area.[13] Clinicians cannot possibly keep abreast of all the literature relevant to their clinical practice without help, and an authoritative synthesis of critically appraised evidence on best practice must be made available at the point of care. Thus, collation of the knowledge base is required, with its delivery to clinicians where and when needed. The National electronic Library for Health[14] is a visionary initiative that aims to pull together reliable knowledge in a form that is easily accessible to both clinicians and patients. Ensuring that it is accessible at the point of care: in the surgery, on the wards, in outpatients, even in the home, remains a challenge for those who are developing the communications infrastructure for the NHS and it is hoped that progress will now be rapid. Achieving this vision demands more than the development of a sophisticated technical infrastructure. Sifting, appraising and reviewing the vast knowledge base of healthcare has been catalysed by the Cochrane collaboration[15] and a cultural shift towards evidence-based medicine,[16] but its presentation to busy clinicians who have inadequate time to talk to patients, let alone keep up to date, remains a problem. The solution is believed to lie in producing trustworthy advice in the form of evidence-based guidelines,[17] but there remains a need to ensure their uptake by those who deliver care. This depends on clinicians being involved in the production of local guidelines and requires active local dissemination, education and support,[18] whether guidelines are made available in paper or electronic form.[19] Thus, organisational development, culture change, education and training all need to move forward, hand in hand with technology.

Evidence-based medicine

Evidence-based medicine has been defined as a requirement for individual clinicians to 'engage in life-long, self-directed learning, so that they remain continually up-to-date with research evidence and offer their patients the best available practice according to that evidence',[16] but challenged by those who champion more medicine-based evidence, which reflects more appropriately the diversity and challenges of care at the 'coal face'.[20] This concept of evidence-based medicine also fails to cope with the complexity of some interventions, where accumulation of evidence is difficult and where managing change requires discussion of options and consensus-building among various stakeholders.[21] These difficulties are highlighted by the complexities of national service frameworks for heterogenous diseases, such as cancer,[22] and situations, such as the management of elderly people.[23] The explosion of information available in electronic form adds further concerns about its validity, and measures of quality are needed.

Information about resources, expertise and access to healthcare is surprisingly sparse at both local and national levels. This information is needed by managers, clinicians and patients, and it must be accurate, updated regularly and available at the point of care. The scarcity of such information implies that the development of organisational record systems seems not to have reached the consciousness of the health service as yet.

The primary purpose of the patient record is to inform and support the management of the individual patient. Secondary purposes include provision of information about activity and quality, by extraction from the record data that can be aggregated. Local uses include research, audit and service planning. National uses currently include: identification of activity and resource use to inform decisions on the level and distribution of funds; the generation of organisational and clinical performance tables; and monitoring trends in diseases and healthcare provision.[24] The inadequacy of central returns in meeting these purposes has long been known.

Edith Körner described how 'inaccuracy, lack of timeliness and certain inherent defects form the core of criticism levelled against NHS information', and this was taken as the main premise for her in-depth study of health services information in 1982.[25] The intention of her recommendations was the promotion of better use of statistical information and healthcare intelligence by those who manage healthcare resources.

Although Mrs Körner left no stone unturned in her efforts to rationalise information services, she worked in an era when clinicians were thought to have no need for information derived from aggregate data about their practice, and thus had no perceived role in either its collection or validation. Since her report, the need for information by clinicians has changed, but the validity of hospital episode statistics is deplorable[26] and culture has remained largely static. Thus, regrettably, clinicians continue to play very little part in the collection or validation of central returns, yet more than ever they need timely, accurate and understandable information about their practice. Already, central returns are being used to inspect clinical performance, and it is proposed that this will develop further with the introduction of appraisal and revalidation.[27] Thus the vision is of timely and accurate information that is of value both to clinicians, who deliver the service, and to those who manage it, derived from data held in records used in day-to-day clinical practice. For such data to be comparable across the NHS, generic systems[3] and common clinical[7,8] and technical standards will be essential.

A vision for the future

Clinicians of the future will receive regular reports of their activities, informing them of the numbers of patients they have treated, the presenting complaints, the diagnoses and the actions they have taken. These reports will also tell clinicians of the effects of their actions on patients, both in terms of change in test results, disease activity scores, adverse events and mortality, and also from the patients' perspective in terms of symptom change and quality of life scores.

This patient focus implies greater patient involvement in data collection,[28] and greater access by patients to computer terminals, both in waiting areas and on wards, in primary and secondary care, where they could review data about their illness and its treatment, and could complete patient-focused question-naires that would enable monitoring of outcome.

Well-informed clinicians will rapidly be able to detect areas of practice that need attention. They will be able to map referral rates to activity, so that they can predict a rising waiting list and deal with it by reconfiguring their services. They will monitor complications and adverse events, to pick up trends at an early stage. They will be able to see whether their practice is deviating from the wisdom held in guidelines, and if they are justified in doing so by the details of the individual case. Clinicians will be able to identify their own educational needs, and monitor the experience and results of those they train. They will be able to search for new knowledge by analysing the details of their own practice, and could participate in rigorously designed randomised controlled trials by providing routinely collected data without the need for additional purpose-designed data collection.[29] They will be able to use information about their practice to plan new services and justify investment in them.[30] Clinicians will also be able to involve individual patients in decisions about their care, enabling them to base decisions on detailed knowledge of the clinician's experience, and likely outcomes or side effects of treatment.[11]

This vision for better information, to underpin the management of both patients and the service, applies equally to primary, secondary and community care. In primary care disparate organisations and accountability of teams pre-sent their own challenges,[31] and the need to blur the interface between these sectors is already clear.[32]

How close are we to achieving this vision? Individual patient records remain a shambles in secondary and community care: largely paper-based, disorganised and useless as a ready source of secondary data.[1,26] Progress has been made towards computerised records in primary care, but these remain largely unipro-fessional, unstandardised and of limited value in the generation of secondary information. In hospitals, automation of the processes that surround clinical records has already achieved great benefits to clinicians in many areas by enabling on-line ordering of tests and viewing of results, electronic prescribing, automatic communication with other professionals and scheduling of proce-dures in discussion with patients. Capturing structured clinical data, in a form that is easily analysed and will yield information that is comparable across the NHS, remains more elusive because it poses far greater challenges that require the definition of standards, education, training and culture change. The health service has not yet moved significantly from a professional culture that is domi-nated by clinical tunnel vision, encouraging professionals to see only the needs of the individual patients in front of them, and unable to set this in the wider context and conflicts of the NHS. The service is also so under-resourced that clinicians are not given the time to make the cognitive effort that will enable them to be more precise in their recording of diagnoses and procedures, as well as the discrete capture of data on other clinical parameters, such as symptoms, signs, problems and complications.

So much for where we want to be, where we are now and the obstructions to getting there. How can the NHS move forward?

Moving the NHS forward

First, clinicians need to be involved – in all aspects of change. Information strategies for the NHS have repeatedly identified the need for operational systems, based on professional–patient interaction, but have each time failed to understand what this meant in terms of system design and implementation, and clinical involvement in information management. Regrettably, Edith Körner missed the opportunity to point out the futility of collecting clinical data in central returns without any involvement of clinicians in the process or in data validation, although she did make clear her view that her data sets were a reluctant interim measure. She was insistent that further developmental work in information culture and application was needed, but this was not progressed by central government, much to her disillusionment[33] (*see* Chapter 1). The continuing problems with hospital episode statistics are probably a direct result of this, and should be an early target for change. Giving clinicians ownership and responsibility for paper records and secondary data extraction would start the culture change that is needed if electronic solutions are to work in the future.[33] It will require resources, but these are already deployed in a discredited network to generate invalid central returns that are so mistrusted that new networks are being created to support national service frameworks for cancer, heart disease, stroke and care of elderly people. It will also require education and training, building on the progress made in the late 1990s, to identify the learning needs in this area.[34] Giving clinicians regular feedback would ensure that their involvement was productive and would engage them further in the process. To ensure compatibility and comparability across professions, sectors, organisations and sites, standards for data and systems are needed.

Much has already been achieved in the development of clinical standards for medical records. The clinical terms project involved more than 2000 clinicians from all disciplines in developing a thesaurus of terms to describe all aspects of health and social care.[35] The delay in translating this clinical thesaurus into a useable coding infrastructure is frustrating, but it is hoped that SNOMED-CT,[36] a collaboration between the NHS Information Authority and the American College of Pathologists, will eventually realise this large piece of the vision jigsaw. It is also hoped that the aborted work of the headings project[8] to define and evaluate common headings acceptable to all professionals in all healthcare domains, will be the foundation for an evidence-based record structure, such as that proposed by the Royal College of Physicians.[37] The episodes of care project[32] described lucidly the severe limitations of the current concepts of discrete consultant- and sector-based episodes, and the far-reaching implications of this must be heeded.

Failure to identify the required functions of the patient record in an electronic environment has long been an inhibition to progress, and has allowed the vision embodied in national strategies to be submerged by short-term managerial needs in terms of resources and contracting. The Academy of Royal Colleges sought to redress this situation by preparing a specification of requirements for clinical systems in secondary care.[38] This process has utilised wide medical consultation and should catalyse debate with other professionals so that multi-professional clinical needs are truly met in the next generation of systems development. The needs of primary care are being addressed through the Primary Care Information Modernisation Programme,[39] but community care remains the poor relation.[40] There is also outstanding work in identifying the minimum data that should be collected routinely to enable monitoring of the quality and quantity of NHS activity without additional data collection processes.

The National Programme for IT in England[41] and *Informing Health Care* in Wales[42] both envisage major progress over the next few years. It is likely that this will be patchy, but if the design of the quilt is clear the patches can fit together without gaps, and if the seamstresses are skilled, the result will be worth waiting for. Above all, it needs partnership – between politicians, who can listen to those who deliver the service; between managers, who acknowledge the primacy of individual patient care in determining the information agenda; and between clinicians, who are prepared not only to change their ways of working but to take on new responsibilities, and to work towards a goal that may not give them immediate benefits.

References

1   Audit Commission (1996) *Setting the Record Straight*. HMSO, London.

2   NHS Executive (1998) *Information for Health. An information strategy for the modern NHS 1998–2005*. NHS Executive, Leeds.

3   Williams JG, Morgan JM, Howlett PJ *et al.* (1993) Let there be light. *British Journal of Health Care Computing* **10**: 30–2.

4   Cancer Dataset Project (2000) Consultation document for cancer dataset version 1.0. NHS Information Authority, Birmingham.

5   *National Service Framework for Ischaemic Heart Disease*. (www.doh.gov.uk/nsf/coronary. htm)

6   Williams JG and Morgan JM (1995) The clinician–information interface. In: RA Greenes, HE Peterson and DJ Protti (eds) *Medinfo '95 Proceedings of the Eighth World Congress on Medical Informatics*. International Medical Informatics Association.

7   Swayne J (1993) A common language of care? *Journal of Interprofessional Care* 7: 29–31.

8   NHS Information Authority (2000) *Headings for Communicating Clinical Information*. NHS Information Authority, Birmingham.

9   France E (1997) The impact of the law on patient confidentiality: likely consequences. In: *The British Computer Society Health Informatics Specialist Group. Current perspectives in health care computing part II*. BJHC Ltd, London.

10   Roberts R, Thomas J, Rigby MJ *et al.* (1997) Practical protection of confidentiality in acute health care In: R Anderson (ed) *Personal Medical Information: security, engineering and ethics, Proceedings of Personal Information Workshop. Cambridge, June 1996*. Springer-Verlag, Berlin. pp. 67–78.

11   Elwyn G (2001) *Shared Decision Making: patient involvement in clinical practice*. PhD Thesis. University of Nijmegen, Nijmegen.

12   Guyatt GH, Feeny DH and Patrick DL (1993) Measuring health-related quality of life. *Annals of Internal Medicine* **118**: 622–9.

13   Deighan M and Hitch S (eds) (1995) *Clinical Effectiveness from Guidelines to Cost-effective Practice*. Department of Health, London.

14   National electronic Library for Health. (www.nelh.nhs.uk)

15   The Cochrane Library. (www.cochrane.co.uk)

16   Sackett DL and Rosenberg WMC (1995) The need for evidence-based medicine. *Journal of the Royal Society of Medicine* **88**: 620–4.

17   Centre for Reviews and Dissemination and Nuffield Institute for Health (1994) Implementing clinical practice guidelines: can guidelines be used to improve clinical practice? *Effective Health Care* 1–12.

18   Oxman AD, Thomson MA, Davis DA *et al.* (1995) No magic bullets: a systematic review of 102 trials of interventions to improve professional practice. *Canadian Medical Association Journal* **153**: 1423–31.

19   School of Postgraduate Studies in Medical and Health Care (2001) *An Assessment of an On-line Clinical Information Service at Morriston Hospital (MOCIS)*. Final report to the Nuffield Trust. University of Wales, Swansea.

20   Knottnerus JA and Dinant GJ (1997) Medicine based evidence: a prerequisite for evidence-based medicine. *BMJ* **315**: 1109–10.

21   School of Postgraduate Studies (2001) *A Practical Guide to Achieving Clinical Effectiveness*. University of Wales, Swansea. (www.rcplondon.ac.uk/college/hiu/educationmaterial. htm)

22   Calman K and Hine D (1995) *A Policy Framework for Commissioning Cancer Services*. Department of Health, London.

23   Department of Health. *National Service Framework for Older People*. (www.doh.gov.uk/ nsf/olderpeople.htm)

24 NHS Executive (1998) *Central Data Collections from the NHS*. Health Service Circular 1998/054. NHS Executive, Leeds.

25 Körner E (1987) *First Report to the Secretary of State of the Steering Group on Health Services Information*. HMSO, London.

26 Williams JG and Mann RY (2002) Hospital episode statistics: time for clinicians to get involved? *Clinical Medicine* **2**: 34–7.

27 Maynard A and Bloor K (2001) Reforming the contract of UK consultants. *BMJ* **322**: 541–3.

28 National Assembly for Wales. *Sharing Clinical Information in the Primary Care Team (SCI-PiCT)*. Cardiff, National Assembly for Wales, Cardiff. (Unpublished).

29 Williams JG, Cheung WY, Cohen D *et al.* (2003) Can randomised trials rely on existing electronic data? A feasibility study to explore the value of routine data in health technology assessment. *Health Technology Assessment* **7**(26).

30 Williams JG (1999) The use of clinical information to help develop new services in a district general hospital. *International Journal of Medical Informatics* **56**: 151–9.

31 Rigby M, Roberts R, Williams J *et al.* (1998) Integrated record keeping as an essential aspect of a primary care led service. *BMJ* **317**: 579–82.

32 Rigby MJ and Williams JG (2000) *Definition of Episodes Project. Collaborative Exercise: final report*. NHS Information Authority, Birmingham.

33 Williams JG and Severs MP (1998) Physicians in the information age: are we keeping pace? *Journal of the Royal College of Physicians London* **32**: 193–4.

34 Severs MP and Pearson C (1999) *Learning to Manage Health Information. A theme for clinical education*. NHSE, Bristol.

35 Williams JG, Ford DV and Yapp TR (1993) Capturing clinical activity: coming to terms with information. *Gut* **34**: 1651–2.

36 NHS Information Authority and American College of Pathologists (2000) *SNOMED Clinical Terms. A Global Leader in Healthcare Terminology*. NHS Information Authority, Birmingham.

37 www.rcplondon.ac.uk/college/hiu/recordsstandards

38 Academy of Medical Royal Colleges Information Group. *Specification of Core Requirements for Clinical Information Systems in Support of Secondary Care*. (www.aomrc.org.uk/ACIG.htm)

39 *Primary Care Information Modernisation Programme*. (www.doh.gov.uk/ipu/whatnew/itevent/tables/infoauditinprimary care.htm)

40 Audit Commission (1997) *Comparing Notes: a study of information management in community trusts*. Audit Commission, London.

41 Department of Health. National Programme for IT in the NHS. http://www.doh.gov.uk/ipu/programme/index.htm

42 Informing Healthcare: transforming healthcare using information and IT (2003) NHS Wales, Welsh Assembly Government.

CHAPTER 7

Information for good governance

Ellie Scrivens

Introduction

NHS organisations produce vast amounts of information for many purposes ranging from central monitoring requirements through to that used for monitoring individual activities. Much of this information is produced for others and little finds its way into the hands of boards for their deliberations. Indeed, boards often struggle to know which data sources to use in order to judge whether their organisations are well managed. However, if they are to meet the requirements now placed upon them by HM Treasury to manage key risks facing their organisations, they need to develop a structured approach to select effective information for assessing whether they have appropriate risk management and controls in place.[1,2]

Edith Körner began the move to investing in information-based management systems that would provide boards with the information to assess the effectiveness of their management activities. The original data sets were products of the understanding of consensus management at that time. With the increasing complexity of the social, political and policy environments in which all organisations, public and private sector, find themselves today, there has been universal recognition of the need to ensure that organisations manage change and risk in a structured and systematic manner. The controls assurance agenda recognises the new information needs of boards in an increasingly complex world.

In 2002, the Department of Health (DoH) produced a mandatory set of reporting requirements for the general management of all NHS organisations. Entitled *The Governance Standard*, the reporting requirements outlined a comprehensive business planning approach for use by boards in the planning and management of health services.[3] Compliance with *The Governance Standard* (*see* box) would be audited by the internal audit service and substantiated by the external audit service.

The Governance Standard

- There are clear *accountability* arrangements in place throughout the organisation.
- The board identifies the needs of stakeholders on an ongoing basis and determines a set of *key objectives and outcomes* for meeting these needs, including how it meets its duty of quality.
- The board ensures that there are proper processes in place to *meet the organisation's objectives and secure delivery of outcomes.*
- The organisation is capable of *meeting its objectives and delivering appropriate outcomes.*
- The organisation learns and improves its performance through continuous monitoring and review of the systems and processes in place for *meeting its objectives and delivering appropriate outcomes.*
- The board ensures that there are proper and independent assurances given on the soundness and effectiveness of the systems and processes in place for *meeting its objective and delivering appropriate outcomes.*
- The board can demonstrate that it has done its *reasonable best to achieve its objectives and outcomes*, including maintenance of a sound and effective system of internal control.

Although NHS organisations had been exhorted to apply the principles of good business planning to their activities for many decades, this was the first time that these principles were a mandatory and full requirement on NHS boards. The arguments behind the genesis of this standard drew on the logic of good governance being promoted simultaneously across the private and public sectors. The logic was derived from principles of good governance, that is, the way in which boards should organise their work to demonstrate accountability in the use of, in the case of the private company, shareholder funds, and in the public sector, taxpayers' money.

The Governance Standard was the key stone of a series of standards promoting risk management in the NHS as part of a programme known as 'controls assurance'.[3] This had begun in 1994 with the introduction of a number of pilot studies to improve risk management in healthcare organisations. At the same time, a set of standards describing the financial requirements placed on NHS organisations was produced. Eighteen organisational standards were added in 1998, each dealing with a specific aspect of responsibility for the safety of patients and staff, where failure to ensure that the requirements of the standards were met could result in harm being caused to patients or to staff, or sanctions being applied to the NHS organisation for failing to act in a responsible manner towards its patients or staff through not complying with legislation or other regulations to protect them. In addition, there was a risk management system standard that provided the framework for the management of risks across the whole organisation, and later, a financial management standard and the governance standard. The finance standard pulled together the original standards, and covered areas relating to financial management, which if ignored could put the organisation at risk. The governance standard provided the strategic overview for the management of business risks across the whole organisation.

Genesis of *The Governance Standard*

Concerns about governance gained momentum in the 1990s, after notable exposures of questionable business practices such as those associated with Robert Maxwell, Barings Bank and others. The conduct of business by private-sector companies came under public scrutiny and, at a time when governments were encouraging the participation of members of the public in share ownership, there was a realisation that companies had to be prepared to demonstrate that they were acting in the best interests of their shareholders and not in their own self-interest. In response, many national accounting bodies, either independently or with their governments, devised requirements for board behaviour. The sentiments of the reports in which these requirements were stated shared a number of similar principles, but the most striking was a requirement that boards should place priority on managing the key risks which threatened their business.

The UK version of this report, colloquially referred to as 'the Turnbull report' after its chairman, Nigel Turnbull, required businesses to assure their shareholders that effective internal control systems were in place within their organisations.[4] The recommendations from this report were incorporated into the Combined Code of the Stock Exchange in 2000 and set the requirements for UK listed public companies, laid down by the Financial Services Authority. Good governance, it was held, requires effective control systems.

So what is an effective control system? Control is the processes in place that an organisation uses to achieve its objectives. In general there are considered to be two sorts of controls within an organisation. 'Hard controls' are the rules and regulations laid down within the organisation to prescribe behaviours. 'Soft controls' are the culture of the organisation, which recognises that there are generally accepted behaviours in place to ensure that the people working within the organisation are clear about the risks that the organisation – and therefore its board – is prepared to tolerate and deal with itself. Risks are therefore the currency of control. Uncontrolled risks help to identify failings in control systems. Managed risks help to identify how well the controls are managed within an organisation. Boards are therefore encouraged to study the management and the treatment of risks by their organisations to ensure that the control systems are in place and functioning effectively.

Risk management, therefore, is inextricably linked to the requirement to develop sound processes of internal control, thereby enabling organisations to sign the assurance statement on internal control:

> Risk management grew out of internal control good practice, and the systems it promotes are designed to give assurance to the Board and key stakeholders that management processes are effective and coherent, and that levels of responsibility and accountability are clearly defined.[5]

The Turnbull report, with its emphasis on internal control, required private companies to embed risk management throughout their organisations. The UK Treasury adopted this approach for its government departments and in 2000 required that all government departments develop a framework for risk management, and also, sign what was referred to as a 'Statement of Internal Control'.[6]

Happily, this development coincided with another government policy to promote modernisation and innovation in the public sector. A series of disastrous central government policy implementations led to recognition of the need to ensure that central government departments were capable of undertaking strategic planning by use of risk management. The unsuccessful launch of the Millennium Dome; the failure of the Passport Office to achieve its targets for turnaround in issuing new passports; and others led to the realisation that risk management was vitally important to the development of new public services.[7]

> Too often Central Government does not assess the risk and walks off the end of a cliff. It does not consider where it is going and when it marches forward it does not manage the risk. Too often, there are no pilot projects, no training and no contingency plans.[8]

However, a review by the Cabinet Office revealed that departments had focused more on better-known risks, such as safety hazards and risks associated with scientific uncertainty, than on the strategic risks of running their core businesses.[9] A National Audit Office survey revealed similar findings, in that government departments focused on minimising financial loss or preventing impropriety rather than on the achievement of broad policy objectives.[7] The result was a concerted move by the Cabinet Office to put pressure on government departments to focus more on the achievement of their objectives by examining the risks to achieving the objectives. In short, the emphasis was moving from simply looking at the management of risks to safety, and moving towards the management of risks to the achievement of the wider policy objectives set for government departments.

A review of risk management by the Public Accounts Committee arrived at a similar conclusion: 'risk management is about ensuring the achievement of outputs and outcomes, and having reliable contingency arrangements to deal with the unexpected which might put service delivery at risk'.[9] But in addition, it was emphasised that risk-taking was a positive and forward-looking process that should be encouraged. Risk management is about' 'changing behaviour and having processes in place which support risk-taking and innovation'.

In the Department of Health, the various messages on broadening the scope of risk management found resonance in the development of the controls assurance project. Begun in 1994, with the advent of improved scrutiny of decision-making through the introduction of audit committees, the controls assurance agenda began to grow by recognising the need for improved patient safety.[10] This was supported by developing of standards to improve the healthcare environment through listing of hard controls covering areas such as fire, buildings, plant and equipment, medical devices, medicines management, etc., and through the development of a standard to cover complaints, incidents or adverse events reporting, etc. The Department of Health took this thinking further by introducing the National Patient Safety Agency in 2001, which was to promote the reporting of incidents and near-misses that could be of use in protecting patients and staff.[11] Risks to health and safety, in their broadest sense, were being addressed. During the same period the risks associated with soft controls also began to develop, in particular those concerning the work of professionals employed within the NHS. Clinical governance, which had as its emphasis the cultural and behavioural aspects of healthcare delivery, emerged to promote greater awareness by clinical staff of risks of clinical activity – to patients and to themselves. The third stage of development arrived with the implementation of Turnbull in the requirements for boards to pull non-clinical and clinical controls, hard and soft together, into a single unified system of internal control that would form the bedrock of governance in the NHS.

The unified system of internal control comprises a number of separate and distinct control systems that thread through an organisation. These all contribute to a single management system, leading to the board, which encompasses all risk-based activities in the NHS – ranging from clinical skills through to the management of estates – all ultimately focusing on the overall goals of the system of healthcare set through the national priorities for healthcare issued by central government.

A call to accountability

Central government requires increased accountability, but there is little agreement as to how this is to be achieved. Under the most recent government initiative for the NHS, enshrined in the document, *Shifting the Balance of Power within the NHS: securing delivery*,[12] there is a commitment to allow NHS organisations to take greater responsibility for controlling their functioning. In this model the role of the centre becomes one of monitoring performance and of ensuring that objectives are achieved. The model has been specified as central standards and policies to be set by the relevant government department and the Department of Health, and the monitoring to be conducted by a new inspection and audit agency.[13] Assistance with implementation will be in the hands of the Modernisation Agency and various other agencies.

However, one problem to be tackled within the new accountability framework is the degree of specification built into the design of both standards and monitoring procedures. It is possible to write standards that are so specific, they dictate precisely how organisations should be structured and should operate. This constrains completely the freedom of local management to determine the best use of services and resources. On the other hand, too few specific standards allows local service development to become unequal, and inequity of service provision flourishes. The appropriate level of control is a very fine balance that needs to be struck by central government implementation at local levels. The search is for what has been described as intelligent accountability:

> Intelligent accountability requires more attention to good governance and fewer fantasies about total control. Good governance is possible only if institutions are allowed some margin for self-governance of a form appropriate to their particular tasks, within a framework of financial and other reporting.[14]

The challenge, therefore, is to use the management of risks, as enshrined in good governance, to ensure that organisations can deliver the services that the public want, in the way the public wants to receive them – that is, safely and securely. Accountability, therefore, is about providing services that the general public can trust, wholly and without thinking. And trust requires that the public, both as taxpayers and consumers of services, is not exposed to risk.

> The range of risks to be addressed is of course very wide – most obviously risks associated with financial decisions but including risks to reputation, environmental risks, risks to health and safety, anything in fact which can adversely impact on business continuity and reduce shareholder value.[15]

By espousing Turnbull, and previous reports on corporate governance including Cadbury, Greenbury and Hampel,[3,16–18] the government has accepted the notion of 'holistic business risk management' and is commending this as a set of sound principles for the corporate governance of risk to deliver the accountability needed within the process of modernising public services.

Information requirements

O'Neill[14] has stated that:

> Serious and effective accountability, I believe, needs to concentrate on good governance, on obligations to tell the truth and needs to seek intelligent accountability. I think it has to fantasise much less about herculean micro-management by means of performance indicators or total transparency. If we want a culture of public service, professionals and public servants must in the end be free to serve the public rather than their paymasters.

Intelligent accountability requires that organisations can manage in such a way as to promote trust between members of the public and the management that provides services to them through the appropriate management of risks. However, although there is a natural desire to live in a 'zero-risk' society, it is not possible to make every activity risk-free. Therefore, society needs to find a mechanism for balancing progressive action with appropriate or acceptable levels of risk. In some cases, individuals must be allowed to determine the extent of risk to which they are exposed. In other cases, individuals are taking risks that can be prevented with relative ease. In the former case, individuals who require invasive clinical interventions must themselves be responsible for assessing risks. Hence the need for appropriate patient information and consent procedures in clinical care. In the latter case, wearing a seat belt is a decision imposed by wider society on those who choose to travel in cars. Society has to determine the extent to which interfering in the lives individuals' exposure to risk is acceptable. Equally, organisations have to decide how much risk they expose individuals to in the course of their actions, and governments have to judge where and when controls should be put on organisations to constrain their risk decisions. An organisation has to determine the extent to which it exposes its staff and its customers to certain risks, for example the possibility of legionella micro-organisms in hospital water tanks. The organisation has to determine the appropriate level of monitoring and maintenance of its water system. The government, however, chooses to regulate the amount of air pollution produced. There is a necessary balance between what is called 'acceptable risk' and the level of control placed upon the actions of all levels of society, from organisations to work units, individual staff, individual consumers. In some cases it is easy to legislate for control, in others it is very difficult, expensive and time-consuming to control the actions of every individual. In some cases, the benefit of freedom of choice is felt to outweigh the risks associated with individual actions. In others, economic benefits outweigh the costs of social control. Tobacco smoking is a very risky behaviour, but society has not chosen to outlaw the production and sale of tobacco. Striking a balance between allowing risks to be taken and controlling to protect against risks is a sensitive and politically complex issue.

Governance is about translating these complex choices to an organisational level. All organisations have to be aware of regulations and controls that are placed upon them. All organisations must be aware of the risks that are being run for their staff, their consumers and their local communities by the actions they undertake. All organisations must accept that they must decide, at every level, where they are creating risks that might cause harm or fail to achieve the purpose for which they were created. Every board has to take responsibility for the risks which are inherent in the business that it runs.

Information for governance

So what is needed for a board to fulfil its duties and obligations concerning intelligent accountability and good governance? The board has to understand the risk domains for which it is responsible. It has to understand the control systems it has in place to manage the risks created by the very fact the organisation exists and actions are conducted in its name. The board has to convey to all staff that they are responsible for ensuring that risks are not taken unnecessarily in any part of the organisation. And the board has to assure itself that all risks are managed in a way that will be acceptable to its stakeholders, its public and its consumers. A model of internal control has been devised to provide a framework for NHS organisations to consider the risks that face them (Figure 7.1).

For an NHS organisation, this means ensuring that all the regulations and laws controlling various aspects of its activities are complied with. The complexity of healthcare organisations means that these are many, covering a wide range of domains from clinical practice to NHS estates. It also means that the wide range of activities that are left open to the discretion of individual staff, senior and junior, and those that are left open to individual patients and carers, are also managed in such a way as to ensure risks are controlled appropriately. Dirigible policies that attempt to control all the actions of every individual are not possible and boards have to rely on the soft controls of professional behaviour and staff commitment to ensure that all actions taken within their provenance are acceptable.

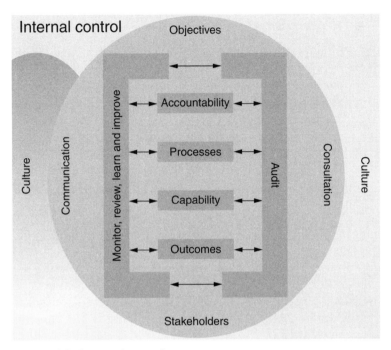

Figure 7.1 A model of internal control.

Monitoring systems are needed to demonstrate that staff are able to review the risks they and their patients face continually, and can account intelligently for the actions that they take when pursuing their professional objectives. Performance measures are needed to inform boards that the right balance is being reached between risk and control. Measures derived from internal management systems, such as complaints and incident reporting, highlight failures within the organisational processes that can suggest where unacceptable risks are being taken. Key performance indicators that focus on the care delivered to patients can show where there are unacceptable risks in the whole service delivery system.[19]

Boards have to determine the nature and the culture of the system of internal control they wish to see within their organisations. They have to be *responsible*, that is, *accountable* for all failures of systems that are designed to ensure that services are adequately and safely delivered to patients and equally that staff are safe and able to work effectively.

Controls assurance has created organisational standards to help NHS organisations deal with some of the obvious risks they face when managing their organisational environments. Other control systems, such as clinical governance, information governance and research governance, are being developed to help to manage specific areas known to present high risks to NHS organisations.

The remainder of the organisation must determine itself through use of behavioural processes. The most commonly used is known as 'control self-assessment', which uses a total quality management-style approach to team assessment of risks in the working environment. Teams are encouraged to review the risks they face in their day-to-day work and to put in place actions and procedures that will help them to manage risks.[20] Risks that need long-term monitoring, or that cannot be solved by the team, are reported to a risk register, which acts as an inventory of risks across the organisation. The risk register can be reviewed by senior management and either acted upon or passed up to higher levels of the organisation for consideration. At each level, significant risks are passed up the organisation and, if serious enough, reach the board for its consideration.

It is common for risk registers also to be used to quantify risk. Each risk is given a probability of occurring (*likelihood*) and a *severity rating* (how serious the outcome would be for the organisation, with death usually being the most serious). In this way, numerical values can be used to determine the degree of significance attached to each risk by the people who identified the risk. Boards are alerted to actions that are of concern within the organisation.

This information has to be put alongside the key performance indicators used by boards to monitor their overall performance. Boards have to learn how to judge the meaning attached to information that is presented, and to decide how to take approriate actions. Board members, who will ultimately be held responsible for the quality of the performance of the organisation, have to exercise their judgement.

Central government, in the form of the Department of Health, can dictate key performance indicators and can dictate the structure of risk management systems. But, in a system with devolved accountability, each and every board has to take responsibility for the actions taken within its organisation. There are no short-cuts to the information required for intelligent accountability. Boards have to provide environments in which staff can operate intelligently, and can communicate freely to ensure that risks are managed. Boards have to have a clear view of their overall direction and their objectives. And boards also have to develop ways of selecting and judging information intelligently to promote a relationship of trust with the general public and other stakeholders.

Edith Körner recognised the need for management information systems to reflect the environments in which healthcare organisations exist, and relate to appropriately, if they are to provide modern healthcare. The NHS modernisation agenda requires an approach to management that is able to deal with a more demanding public, aware of risks to health and with aspirations for the public services that exist to serve them. The governance agenda has advanced to meet these new demands, and in so doing, itself demands a new approach to the use of information to improve the management of healthcare services.

For further information on controls assurance and corporate governance, visit the controls assurance website (casu.org.uk).

Acknowledgement

The NHS Controls Assurance Support Unit is funded by the Department of Health. The views expressed in this chapter are those of the author and not of the Department of Health.

References

1 HM Treasury (2002) *Audit and Accountability in Central Government. The Government's reponse to Lord Sharman's report*. HM Treasury, London.

2 Lord Sharman (2002) *Holding to Account*. HM Treasury, London.

3 Department of Health (2002) *The Governance Standard*. Department of Health, London.

4 The Internal Control Working Party of the Institute of Chartered Accountants in England and Wales (1999) *Internal Control: guidance for directors on the combined code: the Turnbull report*. Institute of Chartered Accountants, London.

5 Minister of Supply and Services Canada (1994) *Quest for Quality in Canadian Health Care*. Health Canada, Canada.

6 HM Treasury (2000) *Corporate Governance: statement on internal control*. DAO(GEN)13/'00.

7 National Audit Office (2000) *Modernising Government – how the NAO are responding*. National Audit Office, London.

8 Sir John Bourne (2002) *Reinforcing Positive Approaches to Risk Management in Government*. Institute of Risk Management, London.

9 Public Accounts Committee (2001) *Managing Risk in Government Departments – first report*. House of Commons, London.

10 Public Audit Forum (2001) *Propriety and Audit in the Public Sector. 1*. Public Audit Forum, London.

11 Department of Health (2000) *An Organisation with a Memory: report of an expert group on learning from adverse events*. The Stationery Office, London.

12 Department of Health (2001) *Shifting the Balance of Power within the NHS: securing delivery*. Department of Health, London.

13 Secretary of State (2002) *Delivering The NHS Plan*. Cm 5503. HMSO, London.

14 O'Neill O (2002) *A Question of Trust*, BBC Reith Lecture, London.

15 Bibbings R (2001) *If it can happen* .... OSH World. http://www.sheilapantry.com/oshworld/focus/2001/200108.html

16 Cadbury A (1992) *The London Stock Exchange. The financial aspects of corporate governance*. Business Science Press, London.

17 Greenbury Committee (1995) *Directors' Remuneration.* Report of a Study Group chaired by Sir Richard Greenbury, London.

18 Hampel Committee (1998) *Committee on Corporate Governance: final report.* The Stock Exchange, London.

19 Wilkes J (2001) How are we doing? *Gasette* **73**: 1–4.

20 Department of Health (2001) *Controls Assurance Project – guidance first principles.* Department of Health, London.

CHAPTER 8

Information for the assessment of health outcomes

Azim Lakhani

Introduction

The Körner reports represent an important stage in the continuing evolution of health services information in the UK. This essay is based on the experience over a decade of the Department of Health's former Central Health Outcomes Unit, and the current outsourced National Centre for Health Outcomes Development, in the use of health services data to assess outcomes – experience in which the vision of Edith Körner has had a significant role.

The National Centre for Health Outcomes Development is a key source of information on assessment of levels of health and outcomes of health interventions, at individual, health authority, NHS hospital trust and local authority levels for the UK National Health Service (NHS) and the government. It is based jointly at the London School of Hygiene and Tropical Medicine, University of London and the Institute of Health Sciences, University of Oxford. In 1993, the Department of Health in England set up the Centre for Health Outcomes Unit to co-ordinate a programme of work to develop methods and systems necessary to assess health outcomes. Following the evolution of a substantial national programme, the unit was contracted out in 1998 and became what is now the National Centre for Health Outcomes Development.

The following is a reflection on three aspects of health outcomes assessment in the NHS:

- What can we do today in the context of what needs to be done?
- What contribution have the Körner reports made to this?
- How can the lessons be applied to fill in gaps?

An approach to the assessment of health outcomes

Health outcome has been defined variously as either a health state at a point in time, or a change over a period, or a result.[1] The National Centre for Health Outcomes Development uses the term 'health' broadly to include health-related status and risk factors affecting health. From the perspective of outcome as a change, there may either be change or no change when change is either expected or not expected. Examples include: no improvement following treatment with antibiotics for an infection when improvement is expected; or activities of daily living of a disabled person not deteriorating. The National Centre for Health Outcomes Development has previously defined health outcomes as changes in health, health-related status or risk factors affecting health, or lack of change when change is expected.[2]

We should recognise that change may occur either by design or through a natural process. The former is more meaningful for performance assessment and health outcome may thus be refined further and presented as a 'result'. The Centre for Health Outcomes Unit defined health outcome as 'attributable effect of an intervention or lack of intervention on a previous health state'.[1] Here, the relationship with the cause of the health state is important. A health state may be the result of an intervention (for example, surgery) or may be due to a known effective intervention not being applied (for example, drug treatment for high blood pressure).

Practical tools for complex concepts – an approach

The home page of the Department of Health's website[3] states simply 'Our aim is to improve health and well-being of people in England'. Assessing success in the context of this aim is, however, no simple matter.[2] Health outcome is often a cumulative result of a variety of influences or services, either provided or not provided, by a variety of organisations over time. The Department of Health is one of many players. In addition to a direct role using its own resources, the Department of Health also has a role in acting as an advocate for health and as a partner with other organisations concerned with health. Any serious attempt at monitoring the achievement of stated health goals should reflect this more complicated reality.

Figure 8.1 illustrates a way of looking at health outcomes as results, drawing a variety of linked health states and services together to provide a summary health outcome overview. It shows further categorisation of 'health improvement' to reflect more specific aspects of outcome, that is, success in:

- reducing level of risk to health
- reducing level of disease and impairment
- reducing adverse consequences of intervention
- reducing adverse consequences of lack of intervention
- restoring function and improving quality of life
- reducing premature deaths.

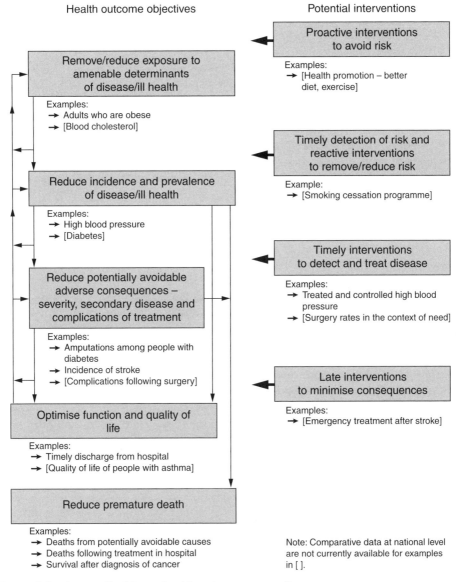

Figure 8.1   A way of looking at health outcomes as results.

Similarly, the action needed to achieve such success is divided into more precise categories:

- proactive interventions to avoid risk to health
- timely detection of risk and removal/reduction of existing risk to health
- timely interventions to detect and treat disease/ill health
- late interventions to minimise consequences of disease/ill health.

This way of presentation helps to clarify and highlight what we are trying to achieve, covering positive aspects, such as improved quality of life, and negative aspects, such as avoidable disease and ill health. It reflects aspects such as clinical signs and disease as well as those of more immediate concern to patients, such as handicap and impact on quality of life. It shows how lack of action may lead to a chain of potentially avoidable consequences, from risk to disease, complications of disease, poor quality of life and premature death, and shows the kinds of action that may alter these consequences for the better. It should be noted that presentation of data in the context of such a 'health outcomes overview' describes mismatching outcomes at a point in time. The data on risk show risk to future health. The data on levels of disease and death show consequences of missed opportunities to reduce risk (if applicable) in the past. It is also not possible to draw direct inferences on 'attributable effects' as there may be different populations involved and a time lag between the interventions and the outcomes. However, such an approach does bring disparate but related items of information together in a meaningful way.

The current state of health outcomes assessment in the NHS using routine data sets

Only a few of these aspects are covered currently by comparative indicators available at national level. Both the Department of Health's *NHS Performance Indicators*[4] and the *Compendium of Clinical and Health Indicators 2001*[5] contain examples of health outcome indicators produced by use of existing health services data, as follows:

- effective action (hip replacements)
- avoidable adverse events (hospital re-admissions, diabetes complications, respiratory infections)
- restoration of function (timely discharge from hospital)
- premature death (deaths after hospital treatment).

Many others are feasible (stroke admissions, gastroenteritis in children). The clinical and health outcomes knowledge base[2] shows how some 150 existing indicators with comparative data may be presented within 29 condition-specific (for example, cancer, diabetes) health outcome overviews, along the lines shown in Figure 8.1. What these charts do show, however, is that coverage is very patchy and has numerous gaps.

These concepts have also been encapsulated in the NHS performance assessment framework.[4] There are two versions of the performance assessment framework for the NHS: one that relates to health authorities and another that relates to provider organisations. There are six areas of performance in the health authority version of the performance assessment framework, aimed at giving a balanced view of performance. Five of these six areas relate to health outcomes. The 'health improvement' area reflects the over-arching aims of improving the overall health of the population and reducing health inequalities that are influenced by many factors reaching well beyond the NHS. The 'effective delivery of appropriate healthcare' area recognises that care must be effective, appropriate and timely, and must comply with agreed standards. Indicators in this area may act as a proxy for health outcomes. For example, if there is good scientific evidence that vaccination is likely to prevent infections then a measure of the coverage of a vaccination programme is an indicator of future health outcomes in terms of infections avoided. 'Fair access' recognises that the NHS contribution must begin by offering fair access to health services in relation to people's needs. This overlaps with effective delivery in that the measures chosen are related to effective processes but act as a proxy for equity of outcomes. The 'patient/carer experience' area reflects the way in which patients and their carers experience and view the quality of the care they receive, including outcomes. The 'health outcomes of NHS care' area covers measures that assess the direct contribution of NHS care to improvements in overall health.

The specific indicators within each area and sub-area will vary from time to time, based on changing policies and priorities. This implies that the main requirement for data is flexibility to meet a variety of needs, often difficult to forecast in advance. Below we see how the vision of Edith Körner contributed to achievements in the assessment of health outcomes within the NHS, based on routine health services data.

The contribution of Körner-inspired principles and procedures to what is possible now

The first report of the Steering Group on Health Services Information, on hospital clinical activity, highlighted the following principles and procedures which have had a direct impact on creation of a data set for the kind of outcomes assessment described above:

- The report was concerned with information for health services management.
- Data should be collected because they are essential for operational purposes.
- User-oriented information yields benefits to those who collect it and thus provides incentives for accuracy and expedition.
- There should be ongoing updating of data specification.
- The logical consequences of these principles are that:
  - central returns should be a by-product of local data
  - local data should be a by-product of operational processes
  - a minimum data set for central purposes represents a compromise between what is desirable, feasible and practical
  - standard definitions and classifications are needed to enable comparison
  - there should be the potential for additional data collection to supplement the minimum specified.

The hospital episodes statistics (HES) data set,[6] which evolved after this report and replaced the previous hospital inpatients enquiry (a 10% sample of regional hospital activity data), embodies these principles and procedures in intent, if not always in practice. HES contain personal, medical and administrative details of all patients admitted to, and treated in, NHS hospitals in England. The records for the database (around 12 million annually) are collected from all hospital NHS trust providers of admitted patient care. There is at least one record for each patient's stay in hospital. The following examples illustrate the current use of HES for outcomes assessment, based on analyses undertaken by the National Centre for Health Outcomes Development for publication as part of the *NHS Performance Indicators*[4] and the *Compendium of Clinical and Health Indicators.*[5]

Effective delivery of appropriate healthcare as a proxy for health outcome

There is research-based evidence to show that hip replacement surgery, if used appropriately, leads to improvements in the quality of life through pain relief and improvement in mobility. The NHS does not collect data routinely on quality of life outcomes among the patients treated within it. However, data on the numbers of operations carried out may be used as a proxy. The operations are carried out in hospital and postcode data from patient records in HES may be used to relate each patient to a health authority of residence and hence calculate population rates of these operations. Figure 8.2 shows that the operation rate among women over 65 years old, resident in health authority areas in England varies threefold. HES are limited in that they do not have data from the private healthcare sector where patients pay for the operations privately. Nor does it have data on criteria for selection of patients for surgery, thresholds for treatment, appropriateness of the operation for individual patients, local waiting list initiatives and local need. It is unlikely, however, that these would explain the levels of variation and the pattern observed.

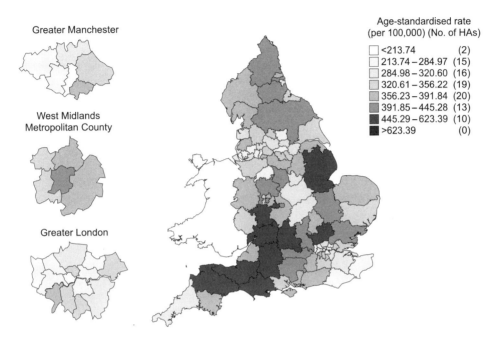

Department of Health. © Crown Copyright. June 2002
Compendium of Clinical and Health Indicators 2001 / Clinical and Health Outcomes Knowledge Base (www.nchod.nhs.uk)
Source of data: Department of Health (Extracts may only be reproduced by permission.)

Figure 8.2　Hospital procedures: primary hip replacement. Directly standardised rates for females (aged 65+), financial year 1999–2000.

Potentially avoidable adverse health events

Lower limb amputations among patients with diabetes may reflect long-term failure of control of diabetes. Ideally, an outcome indicator should be based on the proportions of patients with diabetes who develop such complications. However, there are currently no routine NHS data sets that enable such long-term monitoring. As a proxy, data on patients undergoing amputations in hospital, where diabetes is mentioned as a diagnosis, have been used alongside data on whole populations of health authorities, to develop an indicator. Figure 8.3 shows that there is some threefold variation in the population rates of such amputations. The indicator is constrained because the rate is currently based on whole populations of health authorities, not all patients with diabetes. However, while some of the variation may be explained by differences in the number of people with diabetes in each health authority area, amputations still reflect adverse outcomes as they are potentially avoidable.

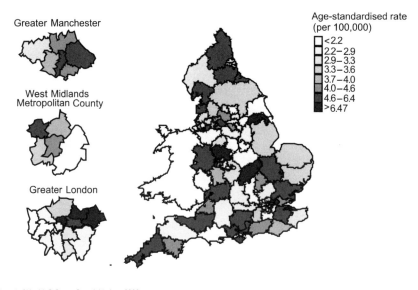

Figure 8.3   Hospital procedures: lower limb amputations in diabetic patients. Directly standardised rates for people of all ages, financial year 1999–2000.

Indicators on emergency re-admission to hospital within 28 days of previous discharge have been part of the clinical outcomes section of the *NHS Performance Indicators* since 1999. These have involved creative use of HES. The basic assumption behind the indicators is that patients are deemed fit for discharge at the time of discharge and a return to hospital as an emergency may reflect unplanned, unforeseen adverse events, some of which may be potentially preventable. There are exceptions to this and in some specialities, for example obstetrics, mental health, conditional discharge and re-admission may be part of planned practice. A patient may be re-admitted to another hospital in another part of the country and thus measurement of re-admissions requires linkage of records for the same patient. This is achieved by assuming that an exact match on three variables between HES records – date of birth, sex and postcode – represents the same patient. The technical details of doing this (subject to ongoing refinement and improvement) are described elsewhere.[4] A variety of indicators has been produced, including ones covering all discharges, either for patients of all ages or specific age groups (children, older people). In addition, indicators have also been produced for individual diagnoses (discharges following emergency admission with hip fracture, stroke). All of these have shown substantial and persistent statistically significant variation in re-admission rates between 'like' hospital trusts, for example small/medium acute, large acute, teaching hospitals, etc. There are a number of constraints with these indicators that are described in the documentation published with the data. However, the indicators raise issues about outcomes which need further local investigation and explanation.

HES has also been used to assess outcomes of care outside hospital, by proxy. The 2002 *NHS Performance Indicators* had an indicator on population rates of emergency admission to hospital for lower respiratory infections among children. Successful prevention, timely diagnosis and treatment may help children to avoid developing problems sufficiently severe to require emergency admission to hospital. The indicator shows fourfold variation in rates of hospital admissions for such infections, with rates in many health authorities significantly higher than the national average.

Restoration of health-related function and quality of life

HES does not have patient level data on health-related function and quality of life. Two indicators were developed to assess this indirectly.[4] The indicators measure the proportion of patients, admitted to hospital as an emergency with hip fractures and strokes, who were discharged to their usual place of residence within a specified time period (28 days for hip fracture, 56 days for stroke). In the absence of routine data on patient levels of function and wellbeing, a return to usual residence following admission with these conditions may act as a proxy for successful outcome of rehabilitation. The category of accommodation as coded in HES is used as a proxy for place of residence. Although the proportion of those who return to pre-admission category of accommodation will depend partly on the availability of support at home and the quality of community services, a change in the category of accommodation may suggest an important change in functional ability and health status. There are substantial variations between 'like' populations and 'like' NHS hospital trusts in the proportions who return to their usual residence. Production of this indicator requires linkage of individual patient episodes into continuous inpatient spells, spanning hospitals across the country. This enables assessment based on the full patient stay, including transfers to other hospitals for rehabilitation before final discharge.

Potentially avoidable premature death

A range of indicators has been produced since 1999 on deaths within 30 days following either an operative procedure in hospital or admission with certain diagnoses.[4] The indicators have been generic (for example, all surgery) as well as operation- (for example, heart by-pass) and condition- (for example, stroke) specific. All have shown variation between 'like' populations and 'like' NHS hospital trusts. In order to measure deaths within a certain time period, it has been necessary to link HES data between trusts as well as with death registration data from the Office for National Statistics. The former enables inclusion of deaths that may occur in a different NHS hospital trust after a transfer. The latter enables inclusion of deaths in the community after discharge from hospital. The techniques used for linkage are described elsewhere.[4] The following results from data at England level for calendar year 2001 show the importance of doing this:

- Of 28 044 deaths after surgery (non-elective admissions), 22 344 occurred within the trust of operation, 851 in another trust and 4849 after discharge from hospital.
- Of 4523 deaths after emergency admission with a hip fracture, 3731 occurred within the trust of admission, 121 in another trust and 671 after discharge from hospital.
- Of 17 629 deaths after emergency admission with a stroke, 16 787 occurred within the trust of admission, 273 in another trust and 569 after discharge from hospital.

Such linkage was constrained because of invalid and missing data in the fields used for linkage, that is, date of birth, sex and postcode, but more sophisticated linkage methods involving the NHS number as well have been used more recently. Linkage of data between years to produce more robust indicators should also be possible in the future.

Current constraints due to failure to follow Körner-inspired principles and procedures

The above examples show what is possible, by way of production of information for management, through the creative use of data collected based on Körner principles and procedures. There are, however, some constraints with such use of data, not owing to problems with the principles and procedures themselves but due to failure to follow them. For example, the National Centre for Health Outcome Development was asked to undertake a feasibility study of producing an indicator on transfer of pregnant women during labour (as an indicator of potentially avoidable adverse events). This required the use of special additional data within HES on mothers and babies. The data for this indicator should be available in the 'baby tail' of the records, one for each delivery. However, the National Centre for Health Outcome Development found that

20% of the baby tail records had missing data and advised that this indicator was not feasible.

Variation in indicator values between hospitals and health authority populations may be due to differences in the types of health conditions and operations carried out, severity of conditions, seriousness of operations and socio-economic characteristics of the patients and populations. HES do not have sufficient information within them to enable adjustment of the indicators to allow for these explanatory factors. A way round this is to compare 'like' with 'like' as far as is possible. For these purposes, hospitals have often been grouped into clusters, for example small and medium acute, teaching, specialised community, and likewise health authorities have been grouped into clusters based on the socio-economic characteristics of their populations. The Körner principle that there should be ongoing review of data sets should help to address this shortcoming over time.

In 1997 the then NHS Executive published a consultation document on potential clinical indicators for the NHS.[7] Among the suggestions were several indicators of complications in hospital following surgery, for example pulmonary embolism (blood clots in the lung), organ damage, wound infections, central nervous system problems, etc. The conclusion following the consultation was that while clinically meaningful as outcome indicators (that is, reflecting potentially avoidable adverse events), the coding of clinical data within HES was insufficiently complete and accurate to make these indicators robust. The Körner principle that there should be ongoing updating of data sets should help to address this shortcoming over time.

There have been improvements to the quality of HES data in recent years. The clinical indicators in the *NHS Performance Indicators* set are accompanied by a detailed assessment for each NHS hospital trust separately, of the completeness of data in all the HES fields used for each indicator. At England level, the percentage of episodes in 1998–1999 that had missing or invalid data in the fields used for the deaths indicators was 5.46 (ranging by trust from 0.06 to 42.5). In 2000–01 this changed to 1.34 (range 0–32.5). In relation to the Körner principles, this has happened not because those collecting data at local level find the data useful, but because those producing management information at central level have exposed deficiencies and made improvements in data completeness mandatory. Trusts are now held accountable for data quality as well as for the results shown by the indicators.

Applying Körner-inspired principles and procedures to filling in gaps

The examples above show that routine national data are severely limited in terms of ability to measure health outcomes precisely. However, creative use of the data has shown that expectations of health outcomes are not being met optimally by the NHS and has raised issues for further investigation. National data will remain limited as it is unlikely that routine data systems will ever be sufficiently detailed and comprehensive to cover all needs and eventualities (although there is room for improvement). However, national comparative indicators should act as a trigger for further work . A number of case studies of follow-up work undertaken by health authorities, following publication of national comparative data on population health outcomes, show the value of this.[2] For example, Sheffield, which had high death rates from coronary heart disease, undertook an angina survey which identified a mismatch between need and service access and led to new service policies. In order to support such local work, 10 working groups, set up by the Department of Health, advised on health outcomes assessment for each of 10 health topics, for example asthma, stroke, and made suggestions for potential health outcome indicators, some of which may require new data collection.[2] Alongside these reports, advice on how to access and use instruments for the measurement of health or health-related quality of life, and information on national clinical databases concerned with more detailed risk-adjusted health outcome indicators are available via the knowledge base.[2]

Table 8.1 shows the kinds of indicators that would be needed to provide a more complete picture of health outcomes for coronary heart disease. The indicators in square brackets are ones that cannot be produced as comparative indicators at national level by use of current routine data. It is remarkable how little can be monitored using routine data at present, given that heart disease is a common health problem and one of the largest single causes of premature death in England. HES cover hospital inpatient care only and are thus limited in terms of coverage of health outcomes. Comprehensive assessment of health outcomes in the context of heart disease would require data on risks, levels of disease, adverse events, quality of life, health promotion, primary care, outpatient care, ambulances, accident and emergency and community care. For example, data from the Health Survey for England show that a proportion of patients with high blood pressure either do not know that they have it or are inadequately treated, with variations between NHS regions.[2] Such indicators could be produced from routine data from the various settings listed, if collected along the same lines as HES. It may even be necessary to link data between settings. For example, production of meaningful health outcome indicators reflecting shared care for heart disease would require the linkage of primary care, hospital outpatient and hospital inpatient data.

Although much of the discussion has focused on central returns and national comparative data, the principles and procedures elicited from the Körner reports did cover local data collection as well. They could be applied to cover data collection for many of the outcome indicators suggested in Table 8.1. Data on the number of patients who get to hospital fast and benefit from early effective

Table 8.1 Health outcome indicators in the context of the NHS performance assessment framework – example coronary heart disease

Performance assessment area and related indicators
  – existing [examples of potential]

Health improvement: the overall health of populations, reflecting social and environmental factors and individual behaviour as well as care provided by the NHS and other agencies

- Success in reducing level of risk to health
  - mean systolic blood pressure
  - mean diastolic blood pressure
  - mean weight of adults
  - mean body mass index (BMI)
  - adults who are overweight
  - adults who are obese
  - smoking of cigarettes, pipes or cigars
  - serum cotinine level above 20 ng/ml
  - alcohol consumption above recommended levels
- Success in reducing level of disease and impairment
  - [coronary heart disease]
- Success in reducing adverse consequences (of intervention)
  - [side effects of risk reduction]
- Success in reducing adverse consequences (of lack of intervention)
  - [heart attacks]
- Success in restoring function and improving quality of life
  - [time off work]
- Success in reducing premature deaths
  - deaths from coronary heart disease
  - deaths from heart disease – other

Fair access: the fairness of the provision of services in relation to need on various dimensions: geographical; socio-economic; demographic (age, ethnicity, sex); and care groups

  – [surgery for heart disease by gender, socio-economic status, age, ethnicity]

Effective delivery of appropriate healthcare: the extent to which services are: clinically effective (evidence-based); appropriate to need; timely; in line with agreed standards; provided according to best practice service organisation; and delivered by appropriately trained and educated staff

- Proactive intervention to avoid risk to health
  - [health promotion initiatives on healthy eating]
- Timely detection of risk; removal/reduction of existing risk to health
  - [smoking cessation services]
- Timely interventions to detect and treat disease or ill-health
  - [surgery for heart disease]
- Late interventions to minimise consequences of disease or ill-health
  - [rehabilitation after a heart attack]

Efficiency: the extent to which the NHS provides efficient services, including: cost per unit of care or outcome; productivity of capital estate; and labour productivity

  – [Cost of surgery]

Table 8.1   *(continued)*

Performance assessment area and related indicators
  – existing [examples of potential]

Patient/carer experience: patient or carer perceptions on the delivery of services, including: responsiveness to individual needs and preferences; the skill, care and continuity of service provision; patient involvement, good information and choice; waiting times and accessibility; the physical environment; and the organisation and courtesy of administrative arrangements

● Patient experience
  – [waiting time for consultation and heart disease surgery]
● Carer experience

Health outcomes of NHS care: the direct contribution of NHS care to improvements in overall health

● Success in reducing level of risk to health
  – [treated and controlled high blood pressure]
● Success in reducing level of disease and impairment
  – [prevention of subsequent heart attacks]
● Success in reducing adverse consequences (of intervention)
  – [complications after surgery for heart disease]
● Success in reducing adverse consequences (of lack of intervention)
  – [time from symptoms to arrival at hospital and thrombolysis]
● Success in restoring function and improving quality of life
  – [quality of life six months after a heart attack]
● Success in reducing premature deaths
  – [sudden deaths caused by heart attacks]

Note: Comparative data at national level are not currently available for examples in [ ].

emergency treatment (thrombolysis) following a heart attack would show local efficiency and effectiveness and could be produced as a by-product of linked operational ambulance and accident/emergency data collection systems.

Conclusions

Sadly, existing data and comparative indicators to monitor health outcomes within the NHS only scratch the surface of what is needed, as set out here. This is because of the complexity of the methods as well as a lack of suitable routine data. The examples presented, however, show what can be achieved through the creative use of routine data. Many of these examples are only possible because of the vision articulated in the reports of the Körner steering group and the evolution of national data systems based on that vision. Extension of that vision to the creation of other data sets at national level could fill in many of the gaps in the ability of the NHS to monitor health outcomes. Further application of the principles and procedures for data collection highlighted in the early

Körner reports could be applied at local level, to supplement national assessment and provide a true comprehensive picture of what is being achieved. Without that, the real return on the vast NHS expenditure will remain in the realms of speculation. The current limited information does show that achievements are far from optimal.

Acknowledgement

The work of the National Centre for Health Outcomes Development is funded by the Department of Health. All views expressed are those of the author and not necessarily of the Department of Health.

References

1 Pearson M, Goldacre M, Coles J *et al.* (eds) (1999) *Health Outcome Indicators: asthma.* Report of a working group to the Department of Health. National Centre for Health Outcomes Development, Oxford.

2 Lakhani A (2000) Assessment of clinical and health outcomes within the National Health Service in England. In: D Leadbeter (ed) *Harnessing Official Statistics.* Radcliffe Medical Press, Oxford.

3 Department of Health (2003) (www.doh.gov.uk)

4 Department of Health (2002) *NHS Performance Indicators: February 2002.* (www.doh.gov.uk/nhsperformanceindicators/2002/)

5 Lakhani A and Olearnik H (eds) (2001) *Compendium of Clinical and Health Indicators, 2001.* National Centre for Health Outcomes Development, London.

6 Statistics Division 2HES (2000) *Hospital Episode Statistics: HES the book.* Department of Health, London.

7 Central Health Outcomes Unit and Statistics Division 2HES (1997) *Clinical Indicators for the NHS (1994–95): a consultation document.* NHS Executive, Leeds.

CHAPTER 9

Principles and purpose for child health informatics

Mitch Blair and Michael Rigby

Introduction

If we define child health as referring to both preventive and curative care delivered from birth to 19 years of age, and informatics as the application of technology and systems to information handling, then it is in the field of child health in the UK where we have seen one of the most successful widespread applications of informatics to healthcare delivery. However, this lead is in danger of being destroyed, and the current benefits lost, as a perverse effect of current and supposedly more integrated strategies.

There are three driving forces behind this. This first is the move towards generic integrated record systems in all settings – primary, community and secondary care; this is a legitimate goal provided there are clear objectives and safeguards, but at present children stand to be disadvantaged as there appears to be a generic adult focus.[1,2] At the same time, existing child health informatics applications are undervalued because their past success has reduced their profile in an era of deficit-correcting strategic informatics investment.

The second is the anxieties raised about the confidentiality and alternative possible uses of large electronically held record systems. However, this type of system has been proved to have been secure and to have benefited children's health in the past, especially in the areas of immunisation and child health screening, and should continue to do so in the future.[3-5]

Third, the experienced NHS bodies best placed to operate such population-based systems, such as health authority and regional NHS bodies, are subject to regular change and destabilisation.[6] NHS reforms are not conducive to the operational stability necessary to create established procedures or the build-up of valuable databases. In order to address these issues positively and constructively, promoting health gain benefits whilst setting an ethical and practical framework, the Royal College of Paediatrics and Child Health (formerly the British Paediatric Association) worked with partner professional organisations involved in child health to foster a constructive dialogue in the context of professional and national policy issues, and to promote clear principles, through an interprofessional forum on child health informatics, co-chaired by the authors. Through these discussions, key principles have emerged, and these are reported here.

Background and context

British child health informatics – a history of benefits

Whilst the collection, recording and communication of relevant information is central to all clinical work, the number of dispersed professionals from a number of different agencies contributing to the health and related care of children, and the involvement of their parents as well, makes child health information an important and challenging area. The first significant developments in child health informatics to address these issues were made 30 years ago, with innovation in West Sussex involving child registration and immunisation,[7,8] with subsequent extension to developmental surveillance[9] and school health in Cheshire. Even from those early days health gain benefits were proven,[10] including greater social equity.[11] The steady uptake of such systems, at least for immunisation functions, coupled with the unification of the NHS in 1974, stimulated the development of the national Child Health System,[12] hitherto one of the most successful and widespread patient-based electronic record systems in the UK, and possibly in any country (covering up to 60% of the children born in England, and all children born in Wales and Northern Ireland). As a result of the widespread use of these computer-based records systems beneficial initiatives such as the monitoring and improvement of immunisation coverage,[13] or audit of screening programmes,[14] have been possible. Edith Körner recognised, and directly involved, this successful experience in the work of her steering group community services,[15] though the child health system has consistently suffered the same central ambivalence to national innovation as was encountered by the steering group.[16] Children have also been beneficiaries in the development of computerised maternity information systems, insofar as these generate records of the neonate, including obstetric history, to a structured format, allowing for improved communication of information in the critical first few weeks of life.

Current informatics policy direction

However, in recent years the potential and affordability of informatics applications in general have increased considerably, and thus in turn so have the realistic and legitimate expectations of health professional staff and managers to be able to harness health computing. The focus, rightly, is on integrated informatics systems, co-ordinated data capture, and optimised feedback of derived information, utilising modern technology. Each of the four home countries of the UK has its own strategic approach to health information systems, but England in particular was early to place emphasis on integrated patient-based records for all clients in community health.[17]

Simultaneously, changes in the structure and management of the NHS have led to new information requirements, including information to support health commissioning and reimbursement. However, even before the necessary and proposed information system developments of one reorganisation can be implemented, the next round of changes is probably going to be announced. The constant rounds of change to support the (in principle) legitimate good of modernisation do have the serious side effect of undermining the information system stability needed to underpin the desired better services.

The resultant threats to child health systems

An adult model strategic philosophy

Thus, this important lead in child health informatics is perversely threatened by recent much-needed moves to strengthen health record and health informatics applications, seeking to address acknowledged deficiencies.[18] Moves to implement generic hospital information systems, bring person-based record keeping into community health, and extend primary care computing, are each being pursued by means of systems which treat all records generically based on the adult model, and principally focused on treatment of illness. This is reflected in the information strategies and requirements to support the national service frameworks – that started off with a largely 'disease'-focused approach.[19–21] Moves toward better management of resources adopt a case-mix approach, which does not effectively support preventive or personally customised longer-term services. Possibly most seriously, projects to redress the past under-development of community health applications have assumed that children's community services and record needs are the same as for adults,[22] when this is not the case. Thus, although child health was the service that pioneered community health informatics, with proven benefits,[7–11] because of subsequent under-recognition of the issues and past successes this is the very client group which will lose out through latest developments.

Underappreciation of existing child health systems

Paradoxically, whilst improved and sophisticated strategic components are being advocated in areas where information capabilities are lacking at present, long-serving systems are being used suboptimally. This is largely because the traditional organisational structure of service delivery causes a focus only on the information interests of the individual provider, at the expense of building up a holistic picture of the whole child (and total child population), and although the moves towards electronic patient records and electronic health resources have much to commend them, they are a long way off universal application, and appear to have little focus on the special issues of preventive child health.

Furthermore, because of the inevitable pressure on scarce resources for information systems, healthcare providers have been least interested in investing further money in developing a system (or informatics area) which has been perceived to operate satisfactorily for 25 years, yet which is threatened organisationally. This lack of necessity for investment in updating a satisfactory system, coupled with operational drift because of the passage of time (particularly through staff turnover not being matched with formal induction and maintenance training) since first implementation together with lack of continuity of ownership and appreciation with repeated organisational change, has resulted in lack of appreciation of the availability and potential value of existing child health databases.[23]

Potential risks and abuses of electronic record systems

At the same time, there have been concerns about the possibility of breach of confidentiality from new types of networked databases.[24–26] Whilst child health electronic records have not been reported victims of any such abuse in the last 30 years, it is nevertheless entirely proper that adherence to full appropriate confidentiality measures should be ensured, but without inadvertent detrimental effects.[27,28]

Recognition of child health issues

These direct and indirect threats mean that a lead area in health informatics is in danger of losing its position, and thereby a priority client group risks being put at a disadvantage by the application of generic solutions that do not meet the particular needs of children. Through interprofessional discussion the unique particular aspects of effective child health services, the resultant special requirements for record keeping, and the use when necessary of information sharing, have each been identified in a way that fits with appropriate informatics application.

Multiple record subjects

First, others are directly involved in the child's health. Children are seen and treated with the support and involvement of their parents, or of a person acting *in loco parentis*. Indeed, the fact that a natural parent is not the supporting adult is itself important, and very sensitive, health information. Clinical information about the mother in pregnancy and the delivery, and genetic information about both biological parents, may be an intrinsic part of the child's clinical history, yet this is primarily confidential information about other people.

Unique data structures

Second, some health monitoring or healthcare delivery needs of children (and their parents) are unique. Developmental and growth problems are best identified early, often requiring sequential recording of defined data sets. These sets must therefore be compiled to clear structures and meaning, in a way which also allows comparison over time, for instance by calculation of growth velocity or completeness of a particular screening or immunisation programme.

Child-centred inter-agency collaboration

Not infrequently, a child's education and social development are influenced by health factors, and an agreed sharing (and updating) of key factors is desirable. Where interagency support is established as necessary to support or protect children with particular needs or risks, sharing of changes to patterns is particularly important – review of reports into service failures shows that breakdown in interagency communication and recording is a major avoidable cause.[29] Thus common meaning, and strictly controlled yet totally effective information-sharing protocols, are essential.

Mandatory data flows

Lastly, there are some information requirements and specific data flows (most being backed by statute or regulation) that are specific to children. In particular, the Public Health Act 1926 (as incorporated into subsequent legislation) prescribes statutory responsibilities and data flows, whereas the Children Act 1989 and the Education Act 1996 each place requirements for interagency working and for the controlled sharing of certain items of information in relation to child protection and special educational needs, respectively. Additionally, there are long-standing requirements for notifying birthweight, and congenital malformations observable at birth, to the Office for National Statistics,[30,31] and health visitors and general practitioners need rapid notification of neonatal discharges regardless of the locality of birth of the child.

Child health recording requirements

There are particular requirements and opportunities for child health informatics. Interprofessional (and thus child-focused) study has identified these requirements as:

- *Foundation-setting* – new records created after birth are intended to last well into a lifetime – these include community health records, primary care records and, where necessary, hospital records; therefore it is important that these foundation records are accurate and meaningful.
- *Timeliness* – activities happen extremely fast in the first eight weeks of life: neonatal examination, selective immunisation with BCG, midwife and health visitor clinical visits and primary care-based screening and immunisation. Information needs to travel with speed and with no loss of accuracy or confidentiality, but also without undue cost.
- *Stability in stress* – parents (particularly first-time parents) will find the birth and neonatal period hectic, challenging to their lifestyle and probably stressful; they may not retain information given to them, and some information they supply later may be inaccurate, therefore the record system itself must act as a focus for accuracy and stability. The introduction of the parent-held child health record for nearly all births in the UK has been one successful response.[32,33]
- *Changes of identity* – at birth, children's forenames may not be known or formally recorded, whilst the surname recorded at the time of birth may not be that chosen for common use thereafter; record systems must be robust enough to cope with this possible change without loss of data or interruption to access (while also being able to accommodate intended complete changes of identity through adoption). The issue of the NHS number at birth will help greatly in tracking infants in these first few weeks, long after the new NHS number is introduced.
- *Statutory data requirements* – there are particular requirements of legislation or regulation including notification to registrars of births, to the Office for

National Statistics concerning birthweight for all children and to the Office for National Statistics for all children with congenital malformations observable at birth, whilst the system of notification of births to proper officers is a statutory requirement.

- *Cross-boundary working* – a significant proportion of births (possibly 30% in some localities) occur outside the health catchment area of residence, requiring rapid information transfer; similarly, many secondary and tertiary care services for ill children are outside their immediate district of residence, yet those providing care need comprehensive and accurate information. Diagnostic support to preventive services such as phenylketonurial (PKU) screening are often provided regionally, giving major information flow problems when strict timeliness is clinically essential.
- *Cross-agency working* – services for children frequently involve social services, and possibly voluntary bodies, to complement healthcare. Education services are involved with all children, including those of pre-school years, and later in life individual schools also have a key role, often without appreciating the importance of health factors.[34,35] Information systems need to be able to support and learn from partner agencies, but within a sound ethical framework – this issue is not unique to child health but has particular special dimensions, not least the involvement of education services.
- *Unique data sets* – data sets concerning children are far from being age-group-specific versions of generic data sets – in the clinical domain, information about the antenatal history, labour and immediate postnatal period consist of unique structures, whereas other special information recording requirements include parental consent to or refusal of procedures such as immunisation. Developmental surveillance records also need a special structure, as does information relating to educational need and the needs of children under the Children Act 1989.
- *Added value of data* – some types of data gain added value by being recorded in a common format in a common record – these include height and weight data, which, when recorded serially, enable calculation of growth velocities against norms, hearing test results and assessments, and information about unscheduled hospital and other clinic attendances that may show patterns if drawn together. For example, repeat non-attendance at hospital outpatients, with a reduced uptake of immunisation and screening coverage, may alert the practitioner to possible neglect.
- *Record of professional interpretation* – certain clinical items may be capable of recording by standard terminology but with the result that this would lose the significant value that can be added either by context or by professional interpretation, for instance a bruise or a burn is not itself unusual or even worthy of recording, but if repeated, if in an unusual position for an accidental cause, or at variance with the explanation given by the parent, may become highly significant.

- *Record as a tool for advocacy* – the health record may frequently support advocacy for children, who in the early years are unable to give their own clinical history – this may range from the value that can be gained from the hospital paediatrician in seeing the full developmental history, as ascertained in a primary care setting, through to seeking to compensate for low motivation of some parents in presenting the child for preventive services, or to identify the aggregate of the full range of treatment obtained by presentation at an intentionally dispersed range of settings. Furthermore, for particular groups of vulnerable children – such as travellers, refugees, those looked after by the local authority or in temporary accommodation – it is often very difficult for the individual health professional to attain the whole picture without a comprehensive health record.
- *Record partnership* – the existence of an integrated child health system personal record for the child has a symbiotic relationship with parent-held records: the central record will ensure the input to the parent-held record is complete, whilst thereafter acting as a backstop should the parent-held record not be presented at consultation.
- *Transient information ownership* – in infancy children are not responsible for their own health information, and a parent or guardian discharges this responsibility, which passes to children as they develop the appropriate maturity in line with the legal ruling from the Gillick case;[36] thus the proprietary interest in (and access to) the record changes from an adult advocate to the data subject at a period which is not temporally defined.

Child health informatics principles

These information requirements set particular challenges. On one hand, they are not adequately met by strategic initiatives in England (and probably not elsewhere). On the other, if met in an unstructured way they could be perceived to encourage casual sharing of sensitive data in an unethical way, in line with the worst fears of those with anxieties as to the abuse of electronic health databases.[24–26] This is certainly not the intention – child health indeed is highly protective of its good record in this respect, and wishes to promote the highest ethical standards, both intrinsically to protect individuals, and also as an essential prerequisite for the consumer trust needed for effective services.

Aware of these unique requirements and expectations of child health informatics, and at the same time very aware that existing national initiatives sponsored by health departments in the UK are not fully addressing (and in some cases explicitly not recognising) these issues, interprofessional discussions have identified the following child health informatics principles (which apply to information held in any medium, paper-based or electronic). These are based upon professional practice, and reflect earlier policy analysis literature.[37,38] They are shown in the box below.

Child health informatics principles

1 *Purposefulness*: Personal health information about children should only be collected for the purpose of delivering care (preventive, supportive or therapeutic).

2 *Enhancement of care*: Data should only be transmitted between healthcare providers (or between agencies) if this will enhance care.

3 *Openness and transparency*: Young persons, parents or legal guardians should have an interest in, and ownership of, the health information recorded about them, and the data items shared as necessary, except in exceptional circumstances.

4 *Third party interests*: Child health records raise particular problems with regard to third parties' identity, involvement and clinical history; specific care must be taken in cases of separation, changed partners, family conflict and other special circumstances, and over the potential for rapid changes to these facts.

5 *Unimpeded transmission*: Information should flow ahead of, or with, the child when authorised by a health professional in the interest of the child for continuity and completeness of care, and normally with the consent of the child or parent.

6 *Comprehensiveness*: Information sets should be comprehensive, which means that a link with prenatal information should be the norm; health information should normally set children in the context of their home and family.

7 *Positive support of health and development*: Health records for children should support the healthy and full development of individuals to the maximum of their potential; sequential observations should be linked so as to identify actual or potential risks of compromised health or development.

8 *Health outcome and health gain*: Both for the benefit of the individual and so as to increase the overall effectiveness of services, regular review must be undertaken to identify health outcome of support to the individual, and the overall health gain to the child population.

9 *Ethical sharing*: Ethical and open means of sharing appropriate data with partner agencies outside health is frequently important in the child's interest, but requires explicit and clear protocols and the sharing of objectives and methods by health, education and social services

for an individual child; if information is being exchanged between two or more agencies with different approaches to confidentiality, the information must be handled in accordance with the most restrictive principles.

10 *Ethical informatics context*: Data should be recorded, stored, transmitted and used according to sound informatics principles; the eight principles within the Data Protection Act 1984, and use of agreed terms, are of particular importance.

Rationale

The intention behind these principles is to give clear guidance to individual system users in daily practice, to trusts and general practices in the use and the selection of systems, and to system developers. It is recognised that given the sensitivity of the topic, it is unreasonable for all to have to discover robust and ethical solutions. These principles are based upon professional practice principles, effective discharge of the duty of care, and the need to protect the interests of children – both for effective and confidential services, and for quality assurance and service development based on robust empirical analysis.

The principles to do not give scope for indiscriminate data sharing or data aggregation, but nor do they cut across the scope of local ethical committees to authorise responsible research. They seek to reflect legal and mandatory requirements in a client-based and practice-relevant way. They balance the need for complete information if healthcare delivery is to be effective, with recognition of the heightened sensitivity of more comprehensive information sets.

Enablement

If these principles are to underpin and enable the restoration of sound child health informatics as a key underpinning plank of local and national health information systems, two sets of action are needed. One is the widespread use of these principles by all interests – this should range from individual health professionals looking for guidance in a specific situation, through to information managers and senior executives establishing corporate strategic frameworks and audited operational policies. The other is the development of supportive informatics initiatives at national level to enable an active child health informatics environment, for instance by the agreement of common terms in areas where they do not yet exist, such as recording of disability and mental health status. Professional bodies could also strengthen practical aspects of educational programmes.

The future imperative

There is a danger of thinking that 25 years' practical experience of running population-based child health information systems is merely a quarter of a century of history rooted in an earlier century. In mere technology terms this is largely true – computing and communications technologies have moved on radically since the national Child Health System was first created, based on even earlier systems of technology which are now redundant. However, progress cannot and should not be measured merely in terms of the rate of advance of new policies based on new technologies – abounding principles need to endure.

The current march to integrated electronic health records, and much more integrated dependence upon electronic recording and delivery support systems in healthcare, is to be commended. However, if the price of that progress is the loss of the practical experience, carefully defined principles, well-honed tools and clearly defined positive benefits of child health computing, it will be in that regard a false progress and society and its children will be the losers.

Neither UK society, nor indeed any other supposedly developed and civilised societies, can be complacent about either the societal or health sector approaches to meeting the needs of children. Not only do serious problems regarding child abuse, and health service delivery failures, continue to arise, but established successes such as high immunisation rates can be threatened by organisational and service development principles which are continually under the pressure of change.

On the one hand, within England there are desirable initiatives such as the development of a national service framework for children. This is firmly intended to protect and improve services to children, but it is important to ensure that the information initiatives which have been well-developed are similarly understood and supported as part of that focus. The UK is one of the many countries which is committed to supporting the United Nations Convention on the Rights of the Child,[39] which not least has specific clauses relating to the right to effective healthcare. To lose the benefits of the specific innovations in child health computing as part of the move towards a generic (and inadvertently adult-focused) electronic record environment could be construed as directly incompatible with honouring that convention.

Conclusion

There is considerable danger that the development of person-based community and other electronic health records will fail to recognise the particular needs – and potential benefits – of child health informatics, while stimulating over-protective safeguards against possible general abuse which would actively disadvantage children.[27] Recent commendable attempts to make good previous deficiencies in information policy perversely may destroy past gains in this field, rather than making progress from the strong baseline. This has stimulated the professional bodies concerned to identify issues, principles and enabling factors which are desirable to address and promote in this regard.

It is intended that consideration and adoption of these principles will inform national policy and development of techniques (particularly terms and outcomes measures); assist system developers in producing more relevant yet sound products; give healthcare organisations a baseline against which to specify and fund information systems in provider organisations; give clear guidance to practitioners; form an important contribution to defining the benchmark of 'reasonable' practice in a technical area; and above all reassure patients and the public. In a fast-moving NHS modernisation and information investment era, these principles do not lose any cogency or relevance – rather, they should provide sound benchmarks to protect the special interests of children's health.

References

1   Dick RS and Steen EB (eds) for Institute of Medicine (1991) *The Computer-based Patient Record – an essential technology for health care*. National Academy Press, Washington DC.

2   NHS Executive (1998) *Information for Health*. NHS Executive, Leeds.

3   Rigby M (1982) Keeping tabs on immunisation. *Health and Social Services Journal* **92**: 1104–5.

4   Rigby M (1983) Clean bill of health for module. *Health and Social Services Journal* **93**: 1444–5.

5   Rigby M (1985) Child health comes of age. *British Journal of Healthcare Computing* **2**: 13–15.

6   Smith J, Walshe K and Hunter D (2001) The 'redisorganisation' of the NHS. *BMJ* **323**: 1262–3.

7   Galloway T McL (1963) Management of vaccination and immunisation procedures by electronic computer. *Medical Officer* **109**: 232.

8   Saunders J (1970) Results and costs of a computer assisted immunisation scheme. *British Journal of Social and Preventive Medicine* **24**: 187–91.

9   Chesham I, Rigby MJ and Shelmerdine HR (1975) Paediatric screening. *Health and Social Services Journal* **85**: 293–4.

10 Bussey AL and Harris AS (1979) Computers and the effectiveness of the measles vaccination campaign. *Community Medicine* **1**: 29–35.

11 Bussey AL and Holmes BS (1978) Immunisation levels and the computer. *Lancet* **i**: 450.

12 Rigby MJ (1987) The National Child Health computer system. In: A Macfarlane (ed) *Progress in Child Health Vol 3*. Churchill Livingstone, Edinburgh.

13 Begg N, Gill ON and White JM (1989) COVER (Cover of Vaccination Evaluated Rapidly) – description of the England and Wales scheme. *Public Health* **103**: 81–9.

14 Streetly A, Grant C, Pollitt RJ *et al.* (1994) Variation in coverage by ethnic group of neonatal (Guthrie) screening programme in south London. *BMJ* **309**: 372–4.

15 Steering Group on Health Services Information (1984) *Fifth Report to the Secretary of State*. HMSO, London.

16 Rigby M (1998) Information in child health management. In: M Rigby, EM Ross and NT Begg *Management for Child Health Services*. Chapman & Hall, London.

17 NHS Management Executive Information Management Group (1993) *An Information Management and Technology Strategy for the NHS in England – getting better with information*. Department of Health, Leeds.

18 Audit Commission (1995) *For Your Information – a study of information management and systems in the acute hospital*. HMSO, London.

19 Department of Health (1999) *National Framework for Mental Health. Modern standards and service models for mental health*. Department of Health, London.

20 Department of Health (2000) *National Service Framework for Coronary Heart Disease*. Department of Health, London.

21 Department of Health (2001) *Diabetes National Service Framework*. Department of Health, London.

22 Bhuptani B, Collier B, Hull M *et al.* (1993) *Community Information Systems for Providers (CISP) System Overview*. NHS Management Executive, Leeds.

23 Rigby MJ and Nolder D (1994) Lessons from a child health system on opportunities and threats to quality from networked record systems. In: F Roger-France, J Noothoven van Goor and K Staer-Johansen (eds) *Case-based Telematic Systems Towards Equity in Health Care (Studies in Health Technology and Informatics Vol. 14)*. IOS Press, Amsterdam.

24 Anderson R (1996) Clinical system security: interim guidelines. *BMJ* **312**: 109–11.

25 Anderson RJ (1996) *Security in Clinical Information Systems*. British Medical Association, London.

26 Jenkins S (1997) Information and the NHS (for me or for them?). In: R Anderson (ed) *Personal Medical Information – security, engineering, and ethics*. Personal information workshop, Cambridge, UK, 21–23 June 1996, *Proceedings*. Springer-Verlag, Berlin.

27 Rigby M (1997) Keeping confidence in confidentiality: linking ethics, efficacy, and opportunity in health care computing – a case study. In: R Anderson (ed) *Personal Medical Information – Security, Engineering, and Ethics*. Personal information workshop, Cambridge, UK, 21–23 June 1996, *Proceedings*. Springer-Verlag, Berlin.

28 Roberts R, Thomas J, Rigby M *et al.* (1997) Practical protection of confidentiality in acute care. In: R Anderson (ed) *Personal Medical Information – security, engineering,*

and ethics. Personal information workshop, Cambridge, UK, 21–23 June 1996, *Proceedings*. Springer-Verlag, Berlin.

29 Noyes P (1991) *Child Abuse – a study of inquiry reports 1980–1989*. HMSO, London.

30 Alberman E (1998) Analysing and promoting the health of children. In: M Rigby, EM Ros and NT Begg. *Management for Child Health Services*. Chapman & Hall, London.

31 Macfarlane A (2000) Birth and maternity statistics. In: D Leadbeter (ed) *Harnessing Official Statistics* (Harnessing Health Information Series). Radcliffe Medical Press, Oxford.

32 Saffin K (1998) Working with parents. In: M Rigby, EM Ross and NT Begg. *Management for Child Health Services*. Chapman & Hall, London.

33 Macfarlane A and Saffin K (1990) Do general practitioners and health visitors like 'parent held' records? *British Journal of General Practice* **41**: 249–51.

34 Polnay L (1995) *Health Needs of School Aged Children – report of a joint working party of the British Paediatric Association*. British Paediatric Association, London.

35 Hall D (ed) (1996) *Health of All Children, Report of the Third Joint Working Party on Child Health Surveillance*. Open University Press, Buckingham.

36 Times Law Report (1985) Gillick v West Norfolk and Wisbech Health Authority. *The Times*, 21 October.

37 Rigby MJ (1981) Child health – a time for better understanding? *Health Trends* **13**: 97–9.

38 Rigby MJ, Tiplady P and Osborne D (1989) Principles, ethics and law in preventive child health. In: B Barber, D Cao and D Quin *et al*. *Medinfo '89, Proceedings of the Sixth Conference on Medical Informatics, Beijing and Singapore 1989*. North Holland, Amsterdam.

39 United Nations (1990) *Convention on The Rights of the Child*. United Nations, New York.

CHAPTER 10

New methods of documenting health visiting practice

June Clark

Preamble

I confess to being a hoarder. In a box of papers that I hadn't touched for years, there it was ... *Steering Group on Health Services Information. Fifth Report to the Secretary of State: a report on the collection and use of information about services for and in the community in the National Health Service*. And tucked inside it was a yellowed paper typed on an old-fashioned typewriter.

9 May 1983

Dear Ms Clark,

As a regular reader (and admirer) of your bi-weekly column, I found the *cri de coeur* in your last article of particular interest. And a matter for concern.

We published in April of this year an Interim Report about information needed by the community health services and we enjoined health authorities to give the report the widest possible circulation among staff delivering those services in order that they may respond to our invitation to comment before our recommendations become final. It is obvious that the report did not reach you.

I now enclose a copy and hope that you will rejoice in the proposals we make for a computer based system ... I shall put you at the top of the list of future users!

(You understand, of course, that our progress in this field will depend on many factors: the view of the Computer Policy Committee, of authorities, of staff and, not least, of Ministers. So we have some way to go.)

Best regards,
Yours sincerely,
E Körner

At the time I was working as a health visitor in Reading and I was also writing a regular column called *Nursing Matters* in a (then) new journal called *The Health Services*. I cannot now find the article, and I cannot remember exactly what I wrote, but I have a pretty good idea, for it seems sometimes that I have been struggling with the same issue for all of the 35 years I have been in and around health visiting: why are our documentation and information systems for health visiting so awful?

I re-read Körner 5 (as it came to be called) with a mixture of sadness and anger. Anger because, almost 20 years on, the situation in documentation in community health services is at least as bad as Körner found it. Sadness because over the years the name Körner became a dirty word in health visiting and 'Körner statistics' became the *bête noire* of community information systems. It was a fate she did not deserve. I am reminded of a comment by the late Sir Roy Griffiths, who suffered a similar fate in respect of his proposals for introducing general management into the NHS: 'Don't blame me,' he said, 'I didn't implement the **** thing!'

A personal journey

It was at exactly the time that Edith Körner's steering group began its work that my own interest in documentation and information systems was beginning. In 1981 I went back to practice as a health visitor after several years out doing research and bringing up my children. Two incidents triggered what has now become 'my obsession'.

Before taking up my new job, I received a Council of Europe Fellowship to look at child health services in Denmark and Finland. For one who had been brought up, as we were in those days, to believe that health visiting was unique to the UK, and that the way we did things was of course the only right way, it was a real eye-opener; many of the things I learnt then transformed my thinking about primary healthcare and changed my practice as a health visitor for ever after.

I remember one visit in particular that I made with a health visitor in Finland. It was to a young mother with a baby of about three months. After the usual greetings, the mother undressed the baby while the health visitor got out the baby's health record – an A4 folder (we were still using those dreadful A5 cards at that time), which she opened at the centile weight charts. The mother already had out the little book which was her parent-held child health record (an idea which was only just dawning then in the UK). The health visitor weighed the baby and recorded the weight both on her own chart and in the mother's book. I could see that the line of the baby's weight was below the printed curve, and I could see that the health visitor looked worried. They talked for a while – of course I could not understand the language, but I could guess the discussion. Then the mother left us for a moment to fetch – guess what – another little book which was her own record from when she was a baby! They compared the two charts, they laughed, they talked a bit more, the health visitor wrote in both the records, then the mother dressed the baby as the health visitor watched, and the visit was ended.

When we got outside I asked the health visitor to tell me about what had been going on. She said that they had talked about the baby's weight and they had made some decisions about changing the baby's feeding, but she was not worried any more because the mother's own weight pattern had been exactly the same when she was a baby. I said that I had never seen records used in this way – remember this was 1981 – but what a great way to teach! The health visitor was surprised and asked me what we did, and I told her.

'Well,' I said, 'we aren't supposed to take records out of the office, but of course if I have four visits to do in a morning I can never remember which baby has had which immunisations, so I do take the records with me. And then when I park the car (yes I had moved on from a bicycle!) I look at the records of the children I am just about to see, and then I do the visit, and then back in the car, I jot down just the most important things so that I won't forget, and then I fill in the rest when I get back to the office.'

Her eyes got wider and wider, and then she said 'You mean you write down things about people without them knowing? But that's unethical!' It was like a blow between the eyes. I had honestly never thought of it that way before.

Some weeks later I started my new job, taking over a caseload where the previous health visitor had left about three months previously. On my first day, at the top of the pile of urgent visits, there was a request to visit an Asian family with a mentally handicapped boy of four, who should be starting school that week, but the forms had still to be completed. When I visited the family at home, I found a mother who spoke no English, holding the boy on her lap while feeding him from a bottle. The 12-year-old daughter who acted as interpreter told me how proud they were of her little brother because he was the only boy in the family and she was the youngest of four daughters. I am sure that I don't have to spell out the implications.

I went back to the office and consulted the child's records. There was a pile six inches high, including letters from various agencies, and one form about immunisations from the Child Health Computer System which was then just beginning. But since they were totally unstructured, after an hour's struggle I still could not find who had done what when, or what the family had been told or had understood about the child's handicap, or what had been planned for him.

So began a period of four years' practice as an ordinary health visitor again, in which I started to think about records and tried to do something about my own. No one was thinking about computers as things clinicians might use for record-keeping – 'the computer' was the thing that sent out these forms about immunisations that you had to fill in and send back to somewhere unknown, and they were always wrong anyway.

I did not know anything about computers either, but I could already see how useful proper records might be for several purposes:

- for continuity of care (taking over from or sharing care with other workers) and to remind myself when the interval between visits might be several months
- as a tool for teaching and for sharing, and for what we now call contracting with clients
- for managing my caseload
- and then when, a few months later, I spent the days between Christmas and New Year struggling to do what were then called 'end of year stats', I realised that if only I had recorded these things as I went along, all I would need to do now was some simple adding up to produce what I now know is aggregated data.

A year later I changed jobs again, into my first senior management post – as Director of Community Nursing Services for West Lambeth Health Authority.

And on my first day, on my desk was the confidential internal report into the death of Jasmine Beckford – one of the first of the many children who have died because the information that could have identified risks and might have saved their lives was held by different workers in different places and was not shared.

Of course it was not very long before I found how difficult it was to make the decisions about planning and resource allocation that I was now required to make when I did not have the information I needed. I knew that the information I needed was there in the heads, and possibly in the records, of the health visitors and district nurses who were my staff, but there was no way I could get at it without doing massive special investigations – for which I had neither time nor resources.

The Körner recommendations were just beginning to be implemented:

> As an indicator of the volume of the service provided, district management needs to know how many contacts took place during a specified period within each community patient care programme. A contact is an event in which a patient is seen by a nurse face-to-face and may be either a clinic attendance or a domiciliary visit. We recommend that all face-to-face contacts be recorded. (Fifth Report, paragraph 6.13)[1]

If only I had known then what I know now about the need to link interventions with the problems to which they referred! To be fair, Körner herself went on to say:

> We recognise that, in workload terms, contacts with patients differ greatly … A simple count of contacts cannot be used as a measure of work done either by individual members of staff or staff groups. (Fifth Report paragraph 6.15)[1]

But the damage was done. That is exactly how the new managerialism of the time measured performance. As W Barker, whose own work, paradoxically, was later to experience the same kind of misinterpretation and misuse, wrote in 1992 in an article entitled 'Measurement of NHS service provision: activity levels or outcomes?':

> The more hyperactive the service the better it is seen to perform . . . For the past decade thinking has been dominated by the Orwellian view of activity: on Animal Farm four legs were good, two legs were bad. For the NHS four operations are good, two are bad. Forty patients at surgery are good, twenty patients are bad. It matters not if a successful GP practice has a strong health promotion focus so that the other twenty are doing more exercise and eating better, and thus have less need of the GP. That is not how health care is measured today.[2]

My own earlier research[3] had already identified the potential for converting actual times to average times to target times, and using these as a measure of health visiting performance described by Young:

> Such target times can thus be estimated for each health visiting activity; if each nurse records weekly the number and type of visits and clinics she carried out, the administrative staff can estimate a weekly target time for each nurse. If the nurse also records her actual weekly time on duty, the weekly target time expressed as a percentage of the actual weekly time can be returned to each nurse as her performance ratio for that week . . . The performance ratios could engender a spirit of competition among the members of a nursing group, but there is no harm in this. As far as the administrative staff is concerned, the ratios would provide a measure of overall nursing performance.[4]

The report that establishing performance targets was followed by an increase of 38% in the amount of visiting (without any change in clinic and school sessional work), taken in conjunction with what Dawtrey in 1977 called the 'weekly liar', perhaps demonstrates the naïvety of this approach.[5] These studies preceded, and were part of, the impetus for the Körner work, but, sadly, the Körner approach exacerbated rather than alleviated it.

By 1991 I had left the health service altogether for higher education (a fugitive from the 1990 round of NHS reforms), but quite independently, I became involved in a project which, although I did not know it at the time, was to be the bridge between my previous concern with documentation and information systems as a practising health visitor, and the work I am doing now.

It was a project headed by the International Council of Nurses to develop an International Classification for Nursing Practice – a kind of International

Classification of Diseases (ICD) for nursing. The American Nurses Association had brought to the International Council of Nurses the problem that in their system of billing for patient care, nursing was not getting proper recognition, financial or otherwise, because information about what nurses do for what conditions, and with what outcomes, was not being included in the computerised information systems and the large databases that were being used for billing and increasingly to meet the new imperatives of identifying and measuring value for money and outcomes of care (it was to be another five or six years before such imperatives crossed the Atlantic). One reason for this problem was the lack of a standardised language to describe nursing phenomena analogous to the languages such as ICD and Procedures Classifications that were in use in medicine.

As we said in our first publication about the project, 'If we cannot name it, we cannot control it, finance it, teach it, research it, or put it into public policy'.[6]

Over the next three or four years I was catapulted into the world of health informatics and information management, standardised languages and clinical information systems, and the electronic patient record. I discovered the North American Nursing Diagnosis Association (NANDA), the work in language and classification systems going on in the University of Iowa, the work of the American Nursing Association on standardised terminologies for nursing and the Nursing Minimum Data Set. Meanwhile in the UK I began to become involved in the work of the NHS Centre for Coding and Classification and the development of the Read Codes and I joined the fringes of the Nursing Terms project.

In 1996 I was awarded a Winston Churchill Fellowship to investigate the development of standardised languages and clinical information systems for nursing in Europe, and a Florence Nightingale Scholarship to do the same in the USA. That sabbatical changed my world view as dramatically as had that visit to Scandinavia 15 years previously.

On my travels around Europe I learnt about the Swedish legislation on medical and nursing documentation and Ehnfors' work there developing of the VIPS system;[7] about the Belgian Minimum Data Set ;[8] and in the Netherlands about William Goosen's work on developing a reference model for nursing information[9] that shows not only how the information system supports clinical, management and policy decisions, but also how the data about patients recorded by nurses as an integral part of their clinical practice (because it is the basis of their clinical decisions) also constitutes the building blocks of the aggregated data that are required for management and policy decisions.

But in the USA I found that things had moved much further. There was tremendous interest in the development of structured and standardised nursing documentation, tremendous investment in IM&T. Lots of places were using computerised patient records, for a variety of purposes, with bedhead terminals in hospitals and laptops in the community. Nurses everywhere recognised the importance of their records and the significance of nursing diagnosis and the nursing minimum data set for aggregated information derived from clinical records. And researchers were using these data for identifying and measuring the outcomes of clinical practice using new techniques of mining the data held in databases.

In my mind, the pieces of the jigsaw puzzle were coming together. The key pieces – the lessons I had now learnt – were already in place:

- the importance, and potential, of records as a source of information
- the need for structure, standardisation and linkage, and how this could be achieved
- the way that management information could be derived from clinical records
- the way that databases could be used for research purposes
- and, in particular, an exciting new approach to the identification and measurement of nursing outcomes, which avoided the problems of the randomised controlled trial.

The final piece of the jigsaw was my appointment to my present post as Professor of Community Nursing in Swansea in 1997 – back to my roots not only in terms of geography and culture, but also back to health visiting and child health. I wanted to work on identifying and measuring the outcomes of nursing practice, using what I had learnt about health informatics and clinical information systems. And the obvious place to start, given my clinical roots and previous research, was with health visiting records.

My vision

Like Martin Luther King, I have a dream:

- *Decision support*: I want all health visitors to be able to use their records in the way I saw that health visitor use them in 1981 in Finland, now not with an A4 paper folder, but with an electronic notebook. I want them to be able, during visits, to call onto the screen everything they need to know to make their assessments and to do what they need to do. That means access not only to things like each child's immunisation record, but other information entered by other agencies, for example hospital admissions, and to be able to see this alongside relevant information about other members of the family.
- *Sharing information with parents*: I want health visitors to be able to share this with the family, to use it for negotiating plans. When health visitors need to teach about something I want them to be able to pull up diagrams and the latest evidence and clinical guidelines. I want them to be able to call up and print off the relevant information for the client on the spot. If they need to refer or to make an appointment I want them to be able to do it there and then by email.

- *The electronic health record*: I want all the relevant data to be stored in the child health system as the electronic patient record that is the beginning of the child's electronic health record, and I want mothers to have and to hold a parent-held child health record that is used by all the agencies that are concerned with their children.
- I want health visitors to record what they do, preferably on site, using standardised language that the computer system will code and store so that later they can review and evaluate their own practice, and so that their data can be aggregated with that of other health visitors to form the database that will provide managers and policy-makers with the information they need for policy and financial decisions.

Everything on my wish list is technically possible now. Most of it I have seen working. The hardware is already available, and getting better and cheaper every day. We have the expertise to develop the software. We now have the knowledge about clinical practice to work with the systems developers to avoid the mistakes and limitations which have given Körner such a bad name.

The bad news is that soon after I arrived in Swansea I went to a local study day on documentation for health visitors, and I found that little had changed since my efforts of the early 1980s. Health visitors were still spending up to three hours a day on filling in multiple forms about every child they visited; still providing statistics for managers which were of little relevance to them and which they resented as a waste of time; still complaining that they could not get back any of the information they put into the child health system. Worse, the burden was dramatically increased by new, legalistically driven demands for documentation about child protection. The concepts of minimum data sets, standardised languages and such like – well documented in the Körner reports 15 years before – were unknown, and the idea that records might actually be useful and not just a necessary but time-consuming chore had not entered anyone's head.

The Swansea 'Omaha project'

My response was to develop what has become known as the 'Omaha project'. This is a developmental project that began in 1998, the original purpose of which was to find a way of identifying and measuring the outcomes of nursing (health visiting) practice through the retrospective analysis of patient records. At this time health visitors, even more than other groups, were under great pressure to demonstrate cost-effectiveness through the demonstration of outcomes.[10] Examination of existing records showed that the health visitors' records consisted of unstructured narrative that could not easily be analysed for this purpose. Examination of the information available about community health services[11] showed that, 20 years after Körner, NHS trusts in Wales had almost no information about what health visitors were doing, how they were doing it, for what clients, for what problems – let alone with what results. In the trust where the project has taken place, health visitors had no access to computers, and very few had even basic skills in IT or information management. The trust had been using a Körner-based system that had been found to be non-'2000-compliant', and had been abandoned. Health visitors were recording the same data, however, on paper forms; altogether 38 different forms were found to be in use. Four years later this situation remains unchanged. Edith Körner would be horrified.

The emphasis of the project therefore shifted into the development of a structured documentation system that would enable the kind of analysis necessary to achieve our original goals to be achieved. Four years on, we have achieved:

- A structured (person-based, problem-oriented) system for documenting patient encounters, that can:
  - provide an epidemiology of patient problems or health issues discussed by health visitors with their clients, which can be presented at the different levels required by individual practitioners in order to prioritise their work, and by managers to plan services
  - identify the professional interventions made in response to the various issues and problems
  - identify outcomes in terms of changes in the status/severity of the problem, and clients' knowledge and behaviour.
- A standardised terminology for expressing problems and health issues, that:
  - is multi-axial
  - is compatible with the emerging SNOMED-CT terminology
  - includes definitions
  - has been validated in use.
- A (still fairly primitive) computerised version, written as a relational database, that:
  - links the record of the patient encounter to other information about the client (individual or family), such as previous encounters, demographic data, standardised assessments
  - enables the individual practitioner to review work with individual clients
  - enables the production of aggregated data for statistical returns, caseload review, etc.

The Omaha system

The project has come to be called the 'Omaha project' because it uses the documentation system that was developed during the 1970s by the Visiting Nursing

Association of Omaha, Nebraska, USA, supported by a series of grants from the US Department of Health and Human Services, as a method of describing and measuring client problems, nursing actions and client outcomes.[12] The Omaha system is a structured problem-oriented documentation system that includes and relates the three elements of the 'problem' (the focus of the intervention), the intervention and change in the client's knowledge, behaviour or health status. Each of these elements is expressed in a standardised and coded terminology. The terminology consists of a problem classification scheme of 44 nursing diagnoses arranged in four domains (environmental, physiological, psycho-social and health-related behaviours), an intervention classification scheme of four categories (assessment, teaching, case management and procedures) and an outcomes rating scale that is used to score the client's knowledge, behaviour and health status. Each element is defined and coded, and the terminology has been recognised for inclusion in the National Library of Medicine's Unified Medical Language System and will therefore be incorporated into the developing SNOMED-CT terminology. The Swansea project has modified and validated the terminology for use in health visiting while retaining compatibility with SNOMED-CT. The system can be used in either a paper-based or a computerised format, as a stand-alone system or (more commonly) as part of an integrated information system. Its validity and reliability have been extensively tested,[12] and it is used in several countries, although the current project is the first time it has been used in the UK.

The Swansea project

The project began in 1998 with a small group of six volunteer health visitors and is still continuing.

In Phase 1, a pilot study undertaken over a period of three months from January to March 1999, 17 health visitors recorded their encounters with families with new babies by use of a specially designed encounter record (described below). The study was small in scale but the results were encouraging, and the group was awarded a Community Practitioners and Health Visitors' Association/Department of Health Centenary Award of £8000, which enabled one member of the project team to be released for one day per week to co-ordinate a larger and more systematic study.

Phase 2 began in November 1999 and finished at the end of July 2000. In this phase 27 health visitors recorded 769 encounters with a wider variety of client groups (205 families), including older people and families with child protection problems, over a period of nine months. Anonymous data from the encounter records were entered into an 'Access' database for analysis. Evaluation also included a questionnaire to the participating health visitors and to a control group of non-participating health visitors, as well as a focus group held at the end of the study.

In Phase 3 a local Sure Start team (a project to provide intensive parenting support to vulnerable families) used the system to record their encounters with clients.

Phase 4 (the Less Paperwork Better Information Project) ran from August 2001 to July 2002. This was a 12-month project funded by the National Assembly for Wales' 'Invest to Save' budget, to develop a computerised prototype or demonstrator. The participants were the health visiting team (two health visitors and one staff nurse) attached to one general practice. In addition to recording the encounter by use of the Omaha system, the system enabled the practitioners to upload onto their laptop computers data from the national child health system about each of the children they were to visit, and a link to the local hospital enabled messaging about children on the health visitors' caseload between the health visitors and the paediatric liason health visitor. In addition to enabling point of contact recording of the encounter, this phase therefore prototyped the use of data to support decision-making and linkage between the community and hospital systems.

Identifying and measuring outcomes

Identifying and measuring outcomes involves a number of conceptual and methodological problems. In the UK the tendency has been to select service outcomes that are easy to measure, such as length of stay, use of other services or patient satisfaction, rather than clinical outcomes, which are often difficult to measure. Measuring the effects of a particular treatment on a disease can be achieved using the 'gold standard' of the randomised controlled trial. These approaches are difficult or impossible in preventive health services. Most of the literature about measuring outcomes in preventive and public health services focuses on the 'big picture' of mortality and morbidity rates using the methods of epidemiology. But the World Health Organization (WHO), among others, has pointed out that in the end quality depends on individual practitioners, and that individual practitioners therefore need feedback on the quality and effectiveness of their own work.[13] This can only be achieved if clinical practitioners get back information about their own practice, so that they can see what works and what needs to be improved.

Donabedian has defined an outcome as:

not simply a measure of health, well-being, or any other state. Rather it is a change in status confidently attributable to antecedent care.[14]

In order to measure an outcome, therefore, three elements are needed:

- the pre-existing condition
- the intervention
- a measure of change in the condition.

In nursing (or health visiting) this means:

- a nursing diagnosis
- a nursing intervention
- a change in the client's knowledge, behaviour or health status related to the nursing diagnosis.

Diagnosis

Many people find the term 'nursing diagnosis' difficult because of the idea that 'diagnosis' refers only to diseases and to a process that is peculiar to medicine. However, the process of diagnosis (that is, identification and labelling of the 'problem') is used by many other professionals, and the diagnostic label which is the end-point of the process refers more generally to the 'condition' that the professional treats: one of the key differences between medicine and nursing is the 'conditions' that each profession diagnoses and treats.[15] In medicine or hospital nursing the diagnostic label usually implies a problem. More commonly in health visiting, which is concerned with normal healthy people, it is a topic to be discussed as part of health promotion. In the Omaha project the term 'nursing diagnosis' is used to describe the topic or health-related issue that is the focus of a health visiting intervention.

Intervention

The intervention is what the health visitor 'does' about the nursing diagnosis that has been identified. In the case of a drug or a specific treatment, it is easier to describe and measure the intervention. Health visiting interventions, such as teaching and support, are far more intangible and difficult to measure.

Client outcomes

In the acute sector outcomes can usually be measured by determining whether a disease has been cured or symptoms have improved. In health visiting the measurement of change is more problematic: in the absence of a defined 'problem', a more appropriate measure of change may be improved knowledge or behaviour, and even in these fields, change may be small and may not be seen for a long time.

Moreover, the three elements are interdependent. Each can be properly understood only in relation to the others (*see* Figure 10.1). Too often in the past, attempts have been made to evaluate health visiting by the measuring of just one of these elements, usually interventions. This was the key criticism of the Körner approach.

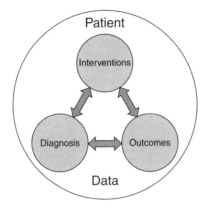

Figure 10.1   The relationship between diagnoses, interventions and outcomes in the client record.

The client record as a source of data

In a randomised control trial these elements are deliberately set up as part of the study. But in fact these elements already exist, or should exist, in the client record. The problem is that sometimes they are not recorded, or if the record is in the form of an unstructured narrative they are difficult to find.

Finding and specifying the three elements and the relationships between them is especially difficult in health visiting. The topics that are the focus of intervention cover a wide range, including both health and social issues, and do not necessarily focus on problems. Sometimes they relate to individuals, sometimes to the family as a unit and sometimes to whole communities. The timescale for identifying change can be very long, spread over many episodes of care, with some issues taking many months, or more commonly years, before they are resolved. The problem of attribution is difficult to determine in any healthcare setting, but becomes even more complex in a preventative service such as health visiting.

Records must be structured so that the three elements can be related, and the concepts must be expressed in a standardised language so like is compared with like. This involves a completely new way of documenting health visiting practice, but it is exactly what the Omaha system is designed to do.

The Swansea Omaha project encounter record

The core of the system, as used in the Swansea project, is the encounter record. In the computerised prototype the encounter module is linked to a registration module, which records identification and demographic data, and an assessment module (not yet developed), which provides for assessments, including standardised assessment tools. The encounter record is a continuous record of health visitors' encounters with a family. It replaces the traditional 'progress notes'. Both paper and computer versions incorporate three sections:

- service details
- topic or nursing diagnosis
- interventions.

The service details recorded include the date, type of contact (for example, home visit, telephone contact, clinic attendance or significant street contact), and a code for Patient's Charter compliance. The computerised version includes who is present during the encounter (important for child protection) and space for emerging performance indicators, which will replace Patient's Charter compliance.

The second section of the encounter record concerns the nursing diagnosis or focus of intervention. Health visitors record each topic, identifying the term and the code from the problem classification scheme. Against each topic they record the 'Bearer' – the client to whom the topic relates (for example, a topic such as 'nutrition' might relate to an individual or to the family as a whole). Next, health visitors judge whether the topic constitutes an actual problem (P), an identified risk (R), or no problem (that is, a topic for health promotion) (N). The acronym PRN has proved easy to remember and code, and enables the record to show the extent of health visitors' health promotion work, which traditional documentation rarely captures. Detail is provided in the the paper version by a second level of classification, and in the computerised version by drop-down lists of signs and symptoms for problems, risk factors in the case of risks and by provision for free text.

Next health visitors score and record the client's knowledge (K), behaviour (B) and health status (S) (acronym KBS) in relation to the particular topic, by use of a simple five-point Likert scale. In Phase 2, participants also recorded the client's level of coping (C) as part of a subproject to test the relevance of coping as a possible outcome indicator. As topics and the client's responses are recorded in successive visits, changes in the PRN and KBS coding provide the measure of change that constitutes the outcome and enables a decision to be made about whether an intervention is working.

Next health visitors record their interventions in relation to each topic. The original version has four broad categories:

- *Assessment* (called 'surveillance' in the original system, and 'monitoring' in the computerised version, but defined to include assessment and monitoring).
- *Teaching* (defined to include guidance and support). In the computerised version this category is divided into two: teaching, and support and counselling.
- *Co-ordination* (called 'case management' in the original system, but defined to include activities such as mobilising resources, arranging referrals, etc.).
- *Procedures and treatments* (less used by health visitors than by district nurses, but defined in Phase 2 of the project to include specific developmental testing, etc.).

An intervention may contain one, two, three or all four of these categories, and can be expanded by a short free-text description.

In the computerised version the intervention section is expanded, using the SNOMED-CT approach, to incorporate details of the focus and the method used (for example under 'monitoring' there is a drop-down list of screening procedures).

Analysing the initial data

Phase 2 enabled the creation of a small database that was used to test the feasibility of analysing the data in ways which would demonstrate the usefulness of the system, in particular the identification and measurement of outcomes. The database can be analysed at any level, for example the individual client, the individual practitioner, a particular locality. Because of the small size of the database, and the limited purpose of demonstrating the potential of the system rather than actual use, the data presented here are aggregations for the whole database.

Epidemiology, needs assessment and service planning

Simple frequency distributions of the problems or issues discussed provide epidemiological data for needs assessment and service planning. Analysis of the most frequently recorded topics (or nursing diagnoses) revealed different trends emerging in different client groups. Tables 10.1, 10.2, and 10.3 show the topics most frequently discussed in encounters with different kinds of clients.

Table 10.1   Topics most frequently discussed in contacts with families beginning at the time of the six-month visit

Topic	No of occurrences	Frequency of occurrence (%) ($n = 89$)	No of occurrences as percentage of all topics recorded ($n = 167$)
Development screening	26	29.2	15.6
Hearing screening	24	27.0	14.4
Vision screening	13	14.6	7.8
Immunisations	7	7.9	4.2
Weaning	6	6.7	3.6
Postnatal depression	5	5.6	3.0
Home or garden safety	5	5.6	3.0

Table 10.2   Topics most frequently discussed in families identified by health visitors as 'cause for concern'

Topic	No of occurrences	Frequency of occurrence (%) ($n = 144$)	Percentage of all topics recorded ($n = 199$)
Weight in relation to centile	9	6.3	4.5
Home or garden safety	7	4.9	3.5
Partner relationships	7	4.9	3.5
Immunisations	7	4.9	3.5
Managing stress	6	4.2	3.0
Development screening	6	4.2	3.0
Failure to carry out important aspects of care	5	3.5	2.5

Table 10.3   Topics most frequently discussed with older people

Topic	Count of topic	Frequency of occurrence (%) ($n = 127$)	No of occurrences as percentage of all topics recorded ($n = 225$)
Range of mobility	20	15.7	8.9
Benefits	15	11.8	7.6
Assuming new role	12	9.5	5.3
Urinary incontinence	10	7.9	4.4
Home or garden safety	9	7.1	4.0
Identifying or mobilising services	9	7.1	4.0
Social contact or social isolation	9	7.1	4.0

The numbers are small, but this analysis does show the potential of the system: if these data were recorded by all health visitors on all families in their caseload, it would give us an epidemiology of health visiting – identifying the kinds of trends and patterns that are familiar to medical epidemiology, not of diseases but of the kind of problems and issues health visitors deal with, which could be used for health needs assessment and service planning.

Each nursing diagnosis or topic discussed is modified by the code P, R or N. When the distribution of PRN codes across an aggregation of all topics discussed is examined, it can be seen that health visitors more frequently identify items for health promotion (that is, N and R) than actual problems (P) as shown in Table 10.4. Previously, this important aspect of the health visitor's role was rarely documented. Certain topics, however (such as benefits, partner relationships, temper tantrums) were usually identified as problems, as shown in Table 10.5.

Table 10.4   Distribution of PRN across all topics

	Problem	Risk	No problem
Frequencies of nursing diagnoses	422 (36%)	241 (20%)	511 (44%)

Table 10.5   Distribution of PRN for selected topics

Nursing diagnosis	Problem	Risk	No problem
Development	9 (9%)	3 (3%)	85 (88%)
Weight	10 (11%)	19 (21%)	63 (68%)
Immunisations	5 (8%)	1 (2%)	53 (90%)
Bottle feeding	8 (18%)	11 (24%)	26 (58%)
Breast feeding	6 (15%)	11 (28%)	33 (57%)
Postnatal depression	17 (59%)	10 (34%)	2 (7%)
Safety	10 (40%)	9 (36%)	6 (24%)
Depression	16 (73%)	5 (23%)	1 (4%)
Benefits	10 (50%)	6 (30%)	4 (20%)

Interventions

The encounter record records the interventions that health visitors undertake. As health visitors perform very few 'hands on' tasks, those outside the profession find it very hard to understand exactly what it is that health visitors do, and health visitors themselves find it very hard to articulate their work. As explained earlier, each topic may provoke one or more than one intervention. Weighing a baby, for example, would usually include all four categories. The physical act of weighing the baby would be recorded as a procedure (P); the health visitor would judge whether the weight gain was appropriate (A); the mother might be counselled about the weight gain (T), and a decision might be made to weigh the baby at clinic next week (C). Table 10.6 shows the frequency of interventions across all topics recorded.

Table 10.6   What do health visitors do?

Intervention	No of occurrences	Percentage of topic records for which this intervention was recorded ($n = 2179$)
Assessment	2126	97.6
Teaching/guidance/counselling	2000	91.8
Co-ordination	1985	91.1
Procedures	673	30.9

Almost all topics include ongoing assessment or monitoring (A), which is one of the most important but least recorded aspects of the health visitor's role. This category is followed closely by teaching and guidance (T). A lot of health visitors' time is also spent on co-ordinating care (C), that is, referring and liasing with other agencies. The figure for procedures is low, and in reality is much lower than the figure suggests because in this phase health visitors were asked to record all 'protocol' visits, such as birth visits, development checks and screening checks as procedures. This was a pragmatic decision because of the complexity of the records required by the trust for such visits. Other than 'protocol' visits, health visitors were asked to record P for any 'hands on' activity, such as demonstrating how to make up a feed or clean a sticky eye as opposed to just discussing it.

Outcomes

Figure 10.2 shows the changes in the status of the problem and in the client's knowledge and behaviour over the database as a whole. This is the first quantitative evidence that health visitors 'make a difference'.

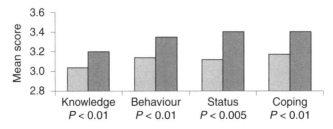

Figure 10.2   Change in mean outcome rating score for all topics

Tables 10.7 and 10.8 show one example taken from the database at a level which individual practitioners might use to monitor their work with a particular client.

Table 10.7   Mother X Topic: *Social isolation* (Code 0601). Database example: change in pre-existing conditions

Date	24/11/99	24/12/99	21/01/00
	P	P	R

Table 10.8   Mother X Topic: *Social isolation* (Code 0601). Database example: Change in client's response

	24/11/99	24/12/99	21/01/00
Knowledge	3	3	3
Behaviour	2	2	4
Status	3	4	4
Coping	3	3	5

The topic being considered is social isolation in a young mother who is the subject of domestic violence and lives in overcrowded conditions with financial problems. Each of these issues would be recorded separately on the encounter record, but in Tables 10.7 and 10.8 only the topic of social isolation is illustrated. It can be seen that on successive visits the Ps (problems) have changed to Rs (risk of problems), showing an improved outcome for this mother in relation to the topic of social isolation. In another family, or for a different topic, it may be possible to see the Ps change to Rs and then to Ns (no problems), demonstrating that a problem had been completely resolved.

Table 10.8 shows the levels of knowledge (K), behaviour (B), status (S) and coping (C) recorded for the same mother and the same topic of social isolation over the same timespan. This gives a more sensitive measure of the change in outcome than PRN, which helps to direct future interventions. For example, it highlights whether interventions need to be focused on knowledge deficit or on providing support to assist in coping skills. In this particular case it can be seen that on 24 November 1999 the lowest score was 2 for behaviour (B). The free text showed that this young mother had isolated herself from her family and friends because of the domestic violence. The health visitor therefore directed her intervention at improving the behaviour, and by 21 January 2000 this score had risen to 4. The free text showed that after counselling by the health visitor the mother renewed contact with her family and friends. As a result, her coping skills had also increased to a maximum score of 5. The health visitor had been unable to take away the risk of domestic violence, but had considerably increased this young mother's ability to cope with the situation she found herself in. This is an outcome that the health visitor would have been aware of before using the Omaha system, but would have found impossible to demonstrate.

Because the Omaha system is a structured and standardised system, it is possible to link these improved outcomes to particular interventions. At the level of individual practitioners it is therefore possible to decide whether an intervention is working or whether it would be helpful to try a different approach. In a larger database the aggregation of data should be able to show, for example, whether levels of behaviour (B) in relation to breast feeding improved following a particular campaign, although very large numbers would be needed to allow the statistical analysis required to demonstrate acceptable levels of probability.

Acceptability of the system to health visitors

A questionnaire was sent at the end of Phase 1 to all the health visitors who had participated in the project. This was analysed in its own right, but was also used as a pilot for the questionnaire sent at the end of Phase 2 to all the health visitors who had participated in that phase of the project and to a control group of health visitors who had not done so. This section relates to the Phase 2 questionnaire.

Twenty-seven questionnaires were sent to the participating health visitors and 20 were returned, a response rate of 74%. Sixty-nine questionnaires were sent to health visitors in the same area who had not participated in the project, and 44 were returned. Health visitors who were using the Omaha system, and those who were not, were first asked about their traditional record system. Then those who were using the Omaha system were asked how it compared with their traditional record system for a variety of factors. The full results are not included here, but Table 10.9 summarises the results of one key question.

Table 10.9 How useful is the Omaha system, compared with your present system, for achieving the following purposes?

	Traditional better (%)	About the same (%)	Omaha system better (%)	Missing (%)
Clinical decision-making	0	30	65	5
Creating a caseload profile	0	25	60	15
Identifying and measuring outcomes	0	5	90	5
Allocation of resources	0	50	45	5
Teaching tool	0	10	80	10
Clinical governance	0	25	70	5

The health visitors overwhelmingly considered the Omaha system to be far better than their traditional record-keeping systems.

Future developments

This is a very small scale project undertaken with very little funding support (a total of £58 000 over five years), but with an enormous amount of enthusiasm and goodwill from its participants. Its significance lies in the fact that the developmental work that has been done on a small scale is a prerequisite for the successful development of any computerised information system and especially for the development and implementation of an electronic health record. We have learnt a great deal about the clinical decision-making that is the core of health visiting practice (as of any professional practice) and how this can be captured in documentation and clinical information systems; for example, we have found that use of a structured documentation system changes clinical practice and improves the focus and specificity of the encounter. Perhaps most important of all, we now understand, and can specify, the requirements for a system that will support practice as well as meeting management requirements – and thus overcome the main criticism of the Körner approach.

Endpiece – visions and progress

A few months ago the gasman came to service my central heating boiler. He put on my kitchen table a little black bag, which he unzipped to reveal a laptop, a baby printer and a mobile phone. Before examining the boiler he pulled up the screen headed 'History' and checked with me when the boiler was last serviced, whether there were any previous problems and so on. On the next screen, 'Assessment', he filled in, in boxes and free text, what he found when he examined the boiler. A widget at the back of the boiler was worn, and he wanted to explain to me why I needed it replaced, so he pulled up a 3-D diagram of the back of the boiler, which I could not see. We agreed that I needed the new part, so he pressed a key to order it from the central depot and said he would be back to fix it in a week's time. When everything was done, he pressed a button on the printer, and put into my hand the printed summary of what we had done, for me to put into – of course – my parent-held gas boiler record.

Now if British Gas can do that for every service engineer, why can't the NHS do it for every health visitor in Wales?

References

1 Steering Group on Health Services Information (1984) *Fifth Report to the Secretary of State*. HMSO, London.

2   Barker W (1992) Measurement of NHS service provision: activity levels or outcomes? *Radical Statistics* 21–9.

3   Clark J (1981) *What Do Health Visitors Do?* Royal College of Nursing, London.

4   Young WC (1971) A work study of nursing staff in a health department. *Health Bulletin* 29: 154–61.

5   Dawtrey E (1977) The Health Visitor in Primary Care. Unpublished MSc thesis. Medical Architecture Research Unit, North London Polytechnic.

6   Clark J and Lang N (1992) Nursing's next advance: an International Classification for Nursing Practice. *International Nursing Review* 29: 109–17.

7   Ehrenberg A, Ehnfors M and Thorell-Ekstrand I (1996) Nursing documentation in patient records: experience of use of the VIPS model. *Journal of Advanced Nursing* 24: 853–67.

8   Sermeus W and Delesie L (1994) The registration of a nursing minimum data set in Belgium: six years of experience. In: S Grobe and E Pluyter-Wenting (eds) *Nursing Informatics: an international overview for nursing in a technological era*. Elsevier, Amsterdam.

9   Goosen W, Epping P and Abraham I (1996) Classification systems in nursing: formalising nursing knowledge and implications for nursing information systems. *Methods of Information in Medicine* 35: 59–71.

10 Roberts C (1996) The proof of the pudding. *Health Service Journal* 14: 27.

11 Clark J (2000) *A Review of Health Visiting and School Nursing Services in Wales*. National Assembly for Wales, Cardiff.

12 Martin K and Scheet N (1992) *The Omaha System: applications for community health nursing*. WB Saunders, Philadelphia.

13 World Health Organization (1999) *Health 21: the health for all policy framework for the WHO European Region*. World Health Organization, Copenhagen.

14 Donabedian A (1988) The quality of care: how can it be measured? *JAMA* 260: 1743–48.

15 American Nurses Association (1980) *Nursing: a social policy statement*. American Nurses Association, Kansas City.

CHAPTER II

Using information for public benefit

Peter Tiplady

Introduction

Modern medical practice is dominated by information. Communication between healthcare staff and patients generates information. Computers and IT process and distribute information that is central to healthcare. Information is what we use to make decisions, and good decisions need information about patients, as well as medical knowledge. The amount of information we need is quite staggering and doctors and nurses spend about two hours every day and about 15% of their budgets on gathering and managing information.

We are only now waking up to the potential of IT and electronic communications to make decision-making easier. We are only now beginning to realise the full potential of sharing this information openly between the healthcare professions, on the one side, and the consumers of healthcare, on the other. We are now at the point of realising the dream of providing equal access to information for clinicians, managers and consumers.

The problems

In the last few years the speciality of informatics has led these developments, but it has to be said that information management in the health service has not had a good record. There has been a poor return on investment in information. The capital costs of installing computer systems in hospitals and surgeries are substantial, and there is no doubt that in the past money has not been spent wisely. Annual maintenance is high; staff training has often been poor; upgrades are expensive and theft of hardware can be a problem. It is sometimes unclear what benefits have resulted from all of this investment, and evaluation of information systems in the NHS has not been good.

It is not just hardware that disappears from hospitals, data disappear too. When information about patients or healthcare staff falls into the wrong hands, either by accident or by deliberate theft, patients become unhappy about their personal data being stored in the computer, staff can imagine that management is spying on them and there is a resulting loss of quality of data until there is a possibility of bad decisions being made.

People need to be able to rely on information systems, and failure can cause clinical problems. However, total system failures are very uncommon, but many health service systems are unreliable and have not been developed with the same rigorous approaches that are usually made in other systems where safety is critical, such as air traffic control.

There are issues here, too for the developing world; the increasing costs of IT could widen the gap between rich and poor countries. Perversely, developments in the Western world could then hinder, or even deny access to information to those in the developing world. At a basic level, the infrastructure to manage information may not be present, and even when it is, the costs of processing and disseminating information may be too great for local economies to bear.

In the West, the availability of huge amounts of health information tempts quasi epidemiologists to go on 'fishing expeditions', particularly in the area of clinical outcome studies, and this kind of unscientific approach brings epidemiology into disrepute.

The benefits

After such a long list of areas where information and computers have had a bad track record in the past, we need to look at examples where there are benefits. Some of these developments have been hindered because of our inability to demonstrate benefit, and in the context of a continuing debate on the confidentiality of health information, it is right that this question has been asked.

Of particular significance to healthcare personnel, in particular clinicians, is the development of relatively inexpensive workstations. The availability of an office suite of software to do word processing, spreadsheet analysis, presentations and database management has empowered healthcare professionals to access and manage data in a way that was unimaginable only 20 years ago. Patient-based information systems with access on a 'need to know' basis are now commonplace. Data can be added to, and analysed, in ways to match individual clinicians' needs and can be developed into management information systems. There are new ways of entering data, which speed up the process for professionals, such as optical character recognition and speech recognition. These developments further 'ownership' of data, and can only lead to improvements in accuracy and comprehensiveness.

Health information and how it is used

The way data about individual patients are now generally stored across several sites poses challenges to their use for public health purposes. Although most systems provide more than adequate access to professionals, it is perhaps only by extending this access to the patients themselves that the highest standards of accuracy could be achieved. The healthcare system tends to have little enthusiasm for sharing data with patients, and patients themselves are increasingly concerned about how their data are handled. In a sense, these concerns are justified when one brings to mind the way the information about individual patients is passed around between healthcare providers, with insurance companies, with researchers, with national statistical offices, with prescription bureaux and the like.

Ordinary members of the public are now managing their bank accounts, their telephone bills, their investments and their purchasing over the internet. They are increasingly turning to on-line sources for information about their health, and consumers will want to see the same access and control for their own medical records. There need to be clear standards developed to guard patients' privacy and those systems should be developed involving patients themselves.

The development of the internet and the world wide web has had a dramatic impact on health informatics. Professionally oriented databases, such as MEDLINE and PubMed, have transformed the way health professionals work. It is perhaps no coincidence that alongside IT developments, evidence-based clinical practice has become the norm. Professionals need almost instant access to the most up-to-date information, and standard textbooks can no longer meet this requirement. Their advice about treatment, prognosis and prevention is frequently out of date before the book is even published. Doctors get better at diagnosis and judgement as they get older, but their knowledge increasingly falls behind. The amount of time available to seek out information for the multitude of clinical problems with which they are presented each day gets less and less. There is simply not enough time in the day to do all of these jobs.

Recent developments in informatics have supported an evidence-based approach to clinical medicine. There are now well developed strategies for tracking down evidence and assessing its quality. Systematic reviews of research and short summaries, such as the Cochrane Collaboration, make sense out of research and lead to better decisions. Most importantly, search strategies and extraction of evidence can now be done through the internet, from wherever one is located in the world.

The same sources of information are available to consumers of healthcare. In the past, health informatics were focused on the needs of the provider. This focus is now moving towards the consumer, a process which is driven by the development of evidence-based clinical practice and the recognition that patients and their carers should have equity of access to information. In Western healthcare systems, the move towards more consumer-focused information bases is partly the result of efforts to control rising healthcare costs by empowering patients to participate in decisions affecting their own health. Patients are now very willing to take on more responsibility for their own health, and the ready availability of information, particularly on the world wide web, is accelerating this change. The new public health agenda emphasises the health of populations as opposed to individuals, and the benefits of primary prevention and the availability of information to both providers and consumers will lead to a new partnership for health, in which consumers use IT to gain access to information about their own health and control their own healthcare utilising scarce resources more efficiently.

It is more than possible that these developments will lead to 'cyber doctors', whose practice is entirely located within cyberspace. There will be a major challenge in regulating the professional practice of a doctor who may not be human. Already in the UK we have NHS Direct, which uses computer algorithms managed by trained staff, to offer a first point of contact to patients. Patients are becoming more and more confident in handling information sources like this, and will increasingly expect immediate access to every kind of information about them or their health.

Every clinician will be familiar with patients or their representatives who come into the clinic with a whole file of information 'off the web'. Whilst doctors, in particular, often find this a threatening process, there are real benefits in patients having access to the same information. Doctors should always remember that patients just might find some information relevant to their condition that they have not come across! The naïve consumer might be seduced by information found on the internet, assuming it to be accurate, up-to-date and valid. This, of course, is far from true, and currently there is no regulation of information on the internet to guarantee safety and efficiency. There are many websites devoted to promulgating information about particular health problems or diseases. The information is frequently unmoderated and lacks peer review. Evidence may be presented without any assessment of its quality and often in a dogmatic style, which gives a false impression of veracity and authority. Organisations like the British Medical Association in the UK are helping enormously by publicising good websites and it is essential that this kind of evaluation is conveyed to consumers. In addition to that, there should be a system of regulating health informatics on the world wide web, probably of a voluntary nature, requiring – among other things – websites to identify authors, their institutions and published peer reviewed articles.

Consumerism in health information empowers patients by giving them access to and control of information. This should include information on their own personal health, such as current diagnostic information, pathology and laboratory results, risk profile, details of prescriptions and untoward effects and so on. Giving patients their medical records is not new, and the idea of a patient-held medical record offers some significant advantages.

The issue of confidentiality meant that in the past, patients did not have access to their medical records. Current UK legislation gives patients access to records made after November 1991 and before that time, if it is necessary for the patient to understand what was written later. There are occasions when access is denied because the doctor feels that some information may be harmful to the patient. Patient-held records circumvent most of the issues about confidentiality and also have enormous practical advantages to both doctors and patients.

Patient access to their own medical records could be achieved either through the internet or through smart cards, or through a combination of both. The smart card would be able to store personal information directly, and would also serve as an electronic key to provide access to information stored elsewhere. Users will be able to find and read their medical records wherever they are, and ensure that information is accurate and timely.

The internet is a vast treasure house of information, but to achieve its full potential users should be pointed in the direction of good-quality information, and websites should instruct them how to assess the quality of information. The internet is notoriously difficult to control, and indeed one of its main attractions is that it is 'uncontrolled'. However, ensuring quality is an urgent priority and cannot be achieved easily. Consumers must be educated in how to phrase questions and search for information to answer those questions. This education could be built into websites; it is unlikely that many people would enrol on a course when they feel that finding information on the internet is so easy. Providers of health information need to regulate themselves and an independent assessor should evaluate their information and issue some kind of 'seal of approval'. A website having this cachet should then be guaranteed high-quality information. Lastly, there need to be sanctions available to stop the distribution of information that is of such poor quality that it could be harmful.

Mention was made earlier of problems in health information in developing countries. There is a well-known story of how Bill Clinton, when President of the USA, visited a village health centre in India. He watched a woman access the world wide web on a computer and get information on how to care for her baby. Writers have retold this story as an illustration of the possibility that this woman would then get better healthcare for her baby because of the availability of information on the internet. This is far from a common situation in developing countries, and on a recent visit to Nigeria I met very few public health colleagues who had any access to the internet themselves, let alone patients. The population of Africa is about 700 million, and less than one million have access to the internet, and eight out of 10 of these individuals are in South Africa. This is probably more representative of the informatics situation in the developing world than what President Clinton saw in India.

Despite the potential value of health informatics in reducing inequalities in the developing world, the sad truth is that the digital divide is more dramatic than any other health inequality. There are very substantial financial barriers to the use of the internet in the developing countries, and in Nigeria a subscription to a service provider and telephone costs are in the region of £500 per annum. In a country where the average earnings are less than a dollar a day, this is a barrier that for most people cannot be breached.

In Nigeria I met professional people delivering primary care of high quality who had no access to literature, no textbooks, no system of recording or analysing information and no method of measuring their progress towards targets. In this sort of environment, public health achievement will be slow. No amount of advice or support from the rich West will make much difference when healthcare professionals and consumers are starved of information. There are some breathtaking IT developments, which could make access to information worldwide. Satellite technology is relatively inexpensive and has already been established in 30 countries, including Asia and Africa. The SatelLife project is supported by the World Bank and is even going beyond communications with sponsorship of a training centre in Kenya where professionals can be taught how to use information technology.

The Untied Nations Millennium Assembly proposed that the right of universal access to information and communication services should be added as a new component of the United Nations principles and conventions on human rights and developments. That right is our responsibility, and it can only be implemented through a truly global initiative to improve access to the internet.

And Edith Körner?

Edith Körner was chair of a steering group that was to re-design the information-gathering system of the NHS and its management use. Sadly, her work was never allowed to be completed, and those of us who worked with her are very much aware that she is remembered in the current NHS largely for a set of data collection forms widely regarded to be unhelpful and tedious; that was never her objective. These are not suitable memorials for Edith Körner. If she had been allowed to complete her work her steering group would by now have moved into developing informatics and information services along the lines that have been outlined in this brief essay. Twenty years on, it is possible to speculate on how many of these proposals would have been well and truly sorted out if she had been allowed to pursue her vision and goal.

CHAPTER 12

Globalisation or localisation: common truths or local knowledge?

Michael Rigby

The work of Edith Körner was commissioned specifically within the UK, and indeed within England. Consequently, most of the essays in this book are rooted in issues of the English healthcare system.

But we are currently in an era of globalisation. Communications, mass media and consequent awareness and expectations mean that news and ideas, and indeed expressed consumer views, travel rapidly around the world. Much of healthcare claims to be evidence-based.[1-4] So, is not the development of locally designed information systems parochial and perverse? Did not Edith Körner's work implicitly draw upon international experience, and are not her principles and her learning points generic and universally applicable? If her work was so seminal, should we not be holding up her guiding principles as universal ideals?

These questions raise a number of important issues. The first of these is the paradox, and the tension, between healthcare delivery and its supposed scientific underpinning. There is a generic desire by the range of stakeholders from consumers to health professionals to base healthcare delivery upon best scientific knowledge and refined expertise. Yet at the same time all stakeholders want healthcare delivery to be localised, both culturally and organisationally – and healthcare information systems are integral to healthcare delivery systems. With the combination of increasingly specialised clinical services and increasing exchange of reference information through modern communications, this focus on localised delivery is looking increasingly difficult, yet is becoming increasingly reinforced.

It is an interesting phenomenon worldwide that healthcare is always a responsibility of devolved levels of government. This is true in the UK, where contrary to international and indeed local indigenous consumer belief, there is no such organisation as the 'British National Health Service'. Within the UK healthcare is devolved to the four home countries of England, Northern Ireland, Scotland and Wales, and with the recently increased amount of devolution those health systems are further diverging, to the point of causing tension because of the differences on specific policy issues. In federal countries such as Canada and Australia the same principle has always applied, with health-care being the responsibility of provincial or state governments. Nor is this a British Commonwealth phenomenon – the same principle of devolved health-care delivery exists for instance in the USA, where it is a state responsibility; Germany, where health is delivered by the Länder; Sweden, where counties are responsible; and Finland, where municipalities are responsible. This under-pins the perceived value of localisation as an important consumer and political principle in healthcare, despite the increasing recognition that many principal therapeutic services, such as trauma and oncology, as well as regional spe-cialities, are best delivered for catchment populations of millions rather than thousands. In the generalist view, sensitivity superimposes on science; commu-nity and culture affect clinical principles.

And that highlights a second fundamentally important point, that scientific truth in healthcare delivery is less universal than is often assumed. And here the consumer paradox works in the reverse direction – the public hears (often through the mass media) of the latest drug development, or surgical innovation, in another country and instantly demands access to it, ahead of any verification of claims, or consideration of the therapeutic effects or the ethical implications within their own local situation.

The importance of local context

Above all, health is a personal issue and a personal demand. But despite the self-survival instinct, which usually assumes that biggest profile means best evi-dence, in fact a range of supposedly objective scientific facts have very different meaning, values, and application at national or local level.

This is an under-recognised issue, which causes difficulty when well-inten-tioned philanthropists or organisations seek to make health knowledge available internationally. Scientific 'fact' from, say, North America or Europe may not be universally applicably within those global regions, and even less applicable in other parts of the world. The proponents of 'knowledge' transfer argue that there are empirical facts that can be grouped together into information and knowledge, which should then be offered on a wider basis to less well-off economies in the interests of the common good. But in fact comparatively few scientific health facts are truly universal. Health and health facts are very per-sonal to the complexity of the human body, to society, to health systems and to cultural values. Thus, any 'scientific' fact requires assessed contextualisation.

Any such 'fact', whether it is scientifically based, such as a drug response, or more related to care delivery, such as the most effective programme of a pattern of care, needs to be contextualised into the local setting because a range of factors need to be take into account to give local context. These can be classified as including the following.

Genetic differences

Not all groupings within the human race have the same physiological or genetic make-up. Different diseases or illness vulnerabilities affect specific groups, often in ways that are not understood, such as the difference in the incidence of cystic fibrosis between Finland and its near neighbours, or the fact that the profile of diabetes in Sardinia replicates that of northern Europe rather than southern. Other factors are well-known, such as vulnerability to sickle cell disease by those of Afro-Caribbean origin, with this trait following communities as they relocate across the globe. Height and body mass also vary by grouping, and so a whole range of tables from growth velocity of infants to pharmacological absorption need to be adjusted for different ethnic groups. And these are just the more obvious differences that are known.

Climatic differences

The human population is distributed from Artic environments to tropical ones; however, much scientific research is based in countries with temperate climates. Many aspects of healthcare are affected by meteorological factors, including temperature and humidity, influencing issues ranging from the best prophylactic approaches to the prevention of pressure sores or to pharmodynamics. In turn, these variations will influence issues such as anticipated length of stay. It is unsafe to assume that research or clinical trial data from one climatic region apply optimally in other climatic regions without adjustment.

Cultural and societal differences

Societies and cultures have different values, many of which are particularly important and precious. These include the role of the extended family varying from being highly active and involved in care to the extent that they take up residence at hospitals and provide patient food, through to the belief in the autonomy and independence of the individual and the expectation that the health system will comprehensively care for their relative – with clear effects upon healthcare delivery patterns and resource assumptions. Other societal and cultural (including religious) beliefs will have major implications for a range of health conditions from teenage pregnancy to the acceptability or otherwise of organ transplants and blood transfusions. These all undermine the assumption of 'universal scientific fact' in clinical and treatment issues.

Health system

There are many types of health system, both with regard to the type of provision being either by the public service, private sector or not-for-profit organisations, and as to whether payment is at the point of consumption, based upon insurance or provided through a tax-funded 'free' public service. These variations in health systems will have major effects upon the information systems needed, and will also affect profiles of delivery patterns. Almost as significant are variations in the interface with other services, not least social welfare systems and social care, but also including housing and education. A health system is not an island, but a focus. And the information it uses needs to recognise the specific local bridges to other services, and the amount and nature of the traffic over them.

Economic status

The healthcare that a country can afford varies tremendously. What is a normal service and reasonable consumer expectation in one country, such as for instance a prosthetic hip replacement or open heart surgery, may be neither physically possible nor economically affordable in another country. At a more mundane level, the availability and affordability of drugs will vary tremendously. Thus many forms of supposedly objective health information, from preferred prescribing patterns to outcome measures, as well as the treatment profiles themselves, vary from country to country, and thus data from one country may not only be irrelevant in another, but actually harmful in that it will skew aspirations or interpretations.

Those issues concern the information contained within systems, the use of supposedly 'universal' scientific facts, and the application of comparative analyses. But what about health information systems themselves, the channels and conveyors of such information? Are there not generic principles that can apply here?

The answer to that must be mixed. And here the legacy of Mrs Körner, and its under-appreciation, applies yet again. Many of the principles that her steering group established apply universally, including the importance of timely and accurate data, and the principle that understanding and relevance must come from the operational levels upwards to the strategic levels. However, almost everywhere the experience is that information systems are developed on precisely the opposite principle – they are designed and imposed on a top-down basis, and the effect is both to load and to disenfranchise the operational levels. This is true in general right across the globe, from highly developed countries to Pacific islands.[5] Second, and linked to this, information systems are usually designed and implemented by those with the resources – namely the central level – with little thought about the views or experience of operational level stakeholders, or concern about meeting their information needs. And, as Mrs Körner discovered to her cost, central sponsors look for quick answers and immediate solutions. Furthermore, they are reluctant to undertake evaluation, and thus refinement and betterment, for a whole range of reasons, including but not restricted to, the desire for minimised investment and also avoidance of loss of credibility.[6]

So, if health information itself cannot be considered universal or global, and if information systems need to be sensitive to local cultures and health systems, is it a sad conclusion that the challenges addressed by Edith Körner have to be replicated in every country? Is there not a place and a means of sharing vision? Fortunately, there are a number of positive ideas that can be put forward, even if the climate is not exactly welcoming because of the expediency and parochialism so often faced.

Rays of light

First, not all countries take the short-term and minimal investment approach that Edith Körner faced. Some countries recognise the importance of developing health information systems, and for doing so in an open and consultative way, with a strong move towards evidence-based and need-based systems. Exemplars of this are Canada, with its strongly supported Canadian Institute for Health Information,[7] and the Commonwealth Government of Australia, with its development of an evidence-based e-health system.[8] This investment in evidence, planning and consultation must surely be beneficial in the longer-term, and the vibrancy of the reports produced by the Canadian Institute for Health Information and Statistics Canada, and the credibility of Australian health information policy documents, would give credence to this.

Second, it ought to be possible to have much better exchange of knowledge and experience about the development of health information systems, and the availability of comparable data. One positive example is within the European Union, where the comparatively new health monitoring programme seeks to provide common analyses of health problems, mortality and morbidity, and health systems' effectiveness across all the member states. There are many problems to be faced in this, given the variety of cultures and health systems across Europe, but it is an ambitious programme which is now well under way.[9]

But on a wider basis, it is highly desirable to share experience of development of information systems themselves, a subject that is currently more restricted to laudable but probably ill-conceived (and sometimes not impartially motivated) drives simply to transfer information systems. Rather than taking this simple transplantation of systems, which will have the unfortunate effect of little local ownership and high probability of limited relevance, it would be much more appropriate to help local opinion leaders and stakeholders to understand the issues and seek to assemble their own structure from experience and components available elsewhere – demand-led rather than donor-driven. This would also reduce the risks of e-colonialism – the imposing by well-off countries of inappropriate information and systems on to the cultures of economically lesser-developed nations through ease of electronic transfer of content without regard to context.

This sharing of experience would probably best be discharged by seeking to assemble learning sets of those who were seeking to develop information systems, and to overlap those with learning sets of those willing to supply ideas or systems but who did not have the same local knowledge of requirement and feasibility. Such learning sets could be focused upon particular common interest constituencies – for instance restructuring countries of Eastern Europe, middle-income countries of Latin America or developing countries in Africa. By coming together on a basis of mutual respect and willingness to learn on a principle of equal standing between both parties (as opposed to any apparent assumption of superior knowledge or status), progress could be made far more constructively. This ought to avoid both the imposition of systems doomed to failure from the beginning (of which there are too many expensive and resource-diverting examples),[10] and instead for each party to develop their thinking based on what they learn across the table from the other.[11]

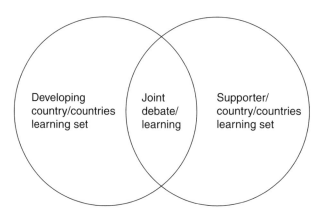

Figure 12.1   A framework for the sharing of experience.

A framework for this has been postulated,[12] as shown in Figure 12.1. A number of potential vehicles exist, not least working groups of the International Medical Informatics Association and its regional affiliates such as the European Federation for Medical Informatics. The most challenging problem is that of finding resources, for either group. For developing or middle-income countries the difficulty of their local experts coming together is self-evident. Unfortunately, it is similarly difficult for potential advisers from more affluent countries to come together in working meetings if there is little possibility of expenses being recouped by commercial sales.

This seems a prime opportunity for funding by appropriate philanthropic bodies, whether these be traditional aid donor agencies, intergovernmental bodies or large private philanthropic trusts. It will be far more effective, because of the associated commitment and thus the enduring nature of the resultant health information systems, if investment is made into this type of learning set and exchange of experience rather than simplistic donation of culturally and organisationally extraneous systems.

Positive examples now exist of organisations seeking to make regionally or culturally customised health information available, usually on the internet, addressed to a particular locality. For example, a charitably underpinned system enables irishhealth.com[13] to publish a regular bulletin summing health information matters relevant to the country of Ireland, specific to its culture, local health problems and healthcare delivery system as well as touching on local health news topics of interest. Quite differently, recognising that much health information at a global level is not directly applicable to the beliefs and cultures of the Arab world, a website has been developed in Saudi Arabia to produce Arab health news.[14] A third example is that of the Eastern Mediterranean Regional Office of the World Health Organization (WHO), which is far more proactive than the other regional offices in seeking to translate selected published material into Arabic for local use.[15]

Conclusion

So having started with the question as to whether the insight into health information as created by Edith Körner and her team, and the related efforts and frustrations they encountered, have to be replicated in every country, the reply must be that there are better ways than this expensive duplication and frustration. However, there is also the dangerous paradox that attempts to share this learning run the great danger of creating the fundamental mistake of turning into global, and top-down imposed, ideas and solutions, when what is actually needed is systems and information that meet local need and respect the issues and values of local healthcare delivery. And in meeting that conclusion it must be reiterated that this was a fundamental principle of Edith Körner herself. So if the adverse learning points of the Körner experience in developing healthcare information systems are to be avoided, the key underlying principle of Edith Körner – the focus on the needs of local healthcare delivery – must be the driving force. In the modern global communications century, the dangers as well as the benefits of instant global health information communication must be assessed in any situation and setting.[16] That suggests three conclusions.

Mutual learning

First, any attitude of proclaiming answers or knowledge from one country to another, and particularly from an affluent global region to areas less well off, must be avoided as not only demeaning, but likely to be irrelevant, ineffectual and thus wasteful of resources.[17] Rather, a context of mutual learning needs to be developed so that local opinion can develop local systems, but based on sound principles and knowledge gained from open discussion and exchange.

Second, any form of information system or information itself needs to be made appropriate for the local setting. Sultan Bahabri, founding Chief Executive of the International e-Health Association, coined the phrase 'glocalisation' for this.[18] This term neatly encapsulates the need to take global information and render it appropriately local. But that too requires resources.

Third, there is no real leadership or vehicle for this localisation process. Though most informed commentators see information as vital to the healthcare process, it is unfortunately the situation that the WHO does not provide strong leadership in this field, though individual programmes, and some of the regional offices, have particular exemplary programmes and strengths. Indeed, some WHO initiatives, such as the HINARI programme of low-cost electronic publishing access to the third world, run the risk of making external and potentially inappropriate information more available in developing countries than appropriate local information.[19]

Global vision of localised systems

Thus there is a need for an approach which brings together the different types and foci of stakeholders, appreciation of their individual values, and an accumulated body of currently scarce evidence as to best types and content of different types of information and media for its supply, so as to develop policies and initiatives. This information and input needs to be from developing countries, and supportive agencies, as much as from the Western world or donors.[20–23]

The International Medical Informatics Association seeks to provide a framework for automated information experience and policy, but has practical difficulty in reaching the underdeveloped and developing worlds. Bodies such as the World Trade Organization and International Telecommunications Union seek to regulate health information activities within those aspects that fall to their own competence. But overall there is a lack of vision of the Körner style at international level. There are no strong vehicles for funding organisational learning as opposed to products, in a way that would be beneficial.

Within the UK, the fact that Edith Körner was an informed visionary has only been learnt slowly over two decades, and the opportunities her work presented in her adoptive country were not taken up at the time. As we move to an era of seeking much greater worldwide understanding of common social and scientific issues, the same situation applies with regards to true global understanding of health information systems. It is an important learning point from the visions Edith Körner provided, and could be a fitting recognition of the deeper contribution she made, if understanding of her approach could be a catalyst to stimulate development of appropriate vehicles for global understanding and resourcing for the building of locally relevant and effective health information systems in countries where they are most needed.

References

1   Cochrane A (1972) *Efficiency and Effectiveness: random reflections on health services*. Nuffield Provincial Hospitals Trust and British Medical Journal, London; printed in revised format, 1989.

2   Davidoff F, Haynes B, Sackett D *et al.* (1995) Evidence-based medicine. *BMJ* **310**: 1085–6.

3   Sackett DL, Richardson WS, Rosenberg W *et al.* (1996) *Evidence-based Medicine: how to practise and teach EBM*. Churchill Livingstone, Edinburgh.

4   Roberts R (1999) *Information for Evidence-based Care* (Harnessing Health Information Series No. 1). Radcliffe Medical Press, Oxford.

5   Finau SA (1994) National Health Information Systems in the Pacific Islands: in search of a future. *Health Policy and Planning* **9**: 161–70.

6   Rigby M (2001) Evaluation: 16 powerful reasons why not to do it – and 6 over-riding imperatives. In: V Patel, R Rogers and R Haux (eds) *Medinfo 2001: Proceedings of the 10th World Congress on Medical Informatics*. IOS Press, Amsterdam.

7   (www.cihi.ca)

8   (www.health.gov.au/healthonline/welcome.htm)

9   (europa.eu.int/comm/health/ph/programmes/monitor/index_en.htm)

10 Rosenow D (2000) Health Management Information Systems Theory and Reality in Developing Countries – A Case Study from the Yemen. Dissertation in part fulfilment for the Degree of MBA (Health, Population and Nutrition), Keele University.

11 Chitalika J (2002) An Assessment of the Need for Computerization of Information Systems at District Level of the Health Sector in Tanzania. Dissertation in part fulfilment for the Degree of MBA (Health, Population and Nutrition), Keele University.

12 Rigby M (2000) Presentation to EFMI Working Group 10 at Medical Informatics Europe Conference, Hanover.

13 (www.irishhealth.com)

14 (www.healthgulf.com)

15 (http://208.48.48.190/his.htm)

16 Rigby M (1999) The management and policy challenges of the globalisation effect of informatics and telemedicine. *Health Policy* **46**: 97–103.

17 Rigby M (2000) And into the 21st century: telecommunications and the global clinic. In: M Rigby, R Roberts and M Thick (eds) *Taking Health Telematics into the 21st Century*. Radcliffe Medical Press, Oxford.

18 Bahabri S (2002) From Telemedicine to e-Health – what's next? Opening presentation to First International e-Health Association Conference and Exhibition 'e-Health 2001', Jeddah, Saudi Arabia.

19 (www.healthinternetwork.org)

20 Arunachalem S (1999) Informatics in clinical practice in developing countries: still early days. *BMJ* **319**: 1297.

21 Tan-Torres Edejer T (2000) Disseminating health information in developing countries: the role of the internet. *BMJ* **321**: 797–800.

22 Costello A and Zumla A (2000) Moving to research partnerships in developing countries. *BMJ* **321**: 827–9.

23 Lam CLK (2000) Knowledge can flow from developing to developed countries. *BMJ* **321**: 830.

Index